DISK
117

IMAGE
0016

OBJECT
MOON, MARIA

FILTER
B

EXP. TIME
0.1

MOUNTAIN DAYLIGHT TIME
03:54:57

EPOCH
1994.5

RA EQUIV. LONGITUDE
23,00,48

DEC EQUIV. LATITUDE
-02,12,00

COMMENTS
TELESCOPE IS 24"DIAMETER
F RATIO 15:2
OPERATING ON RCA CCD

D0820136

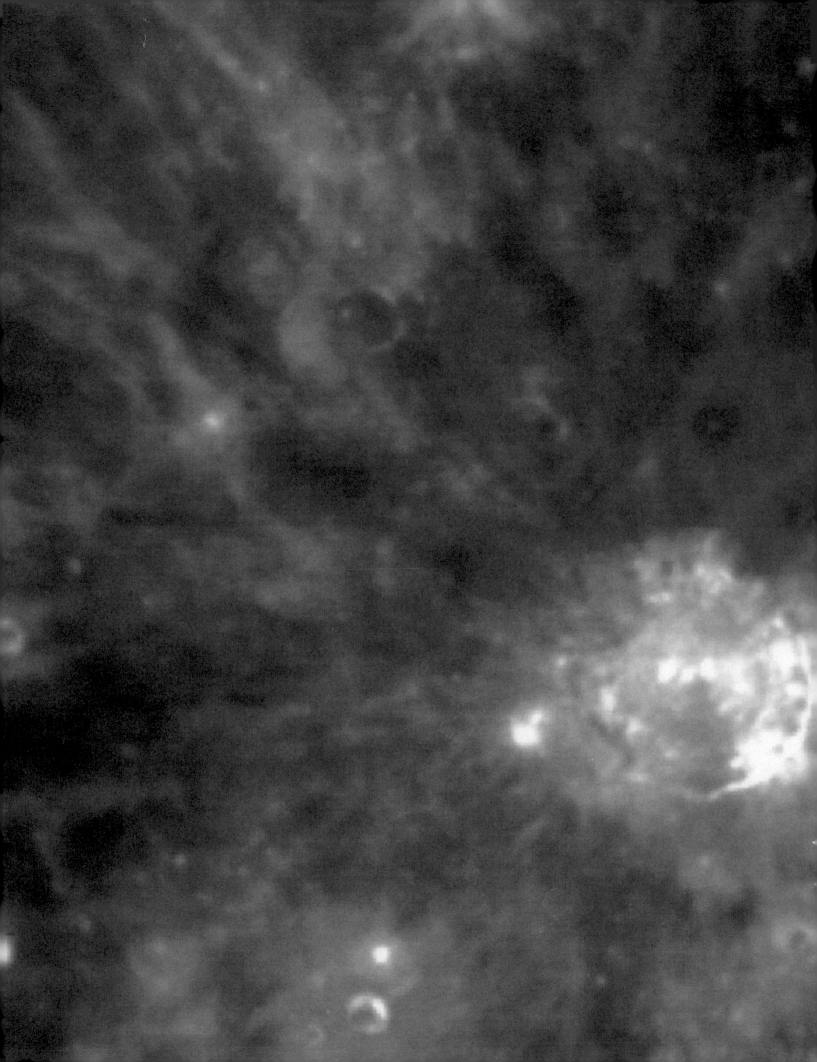

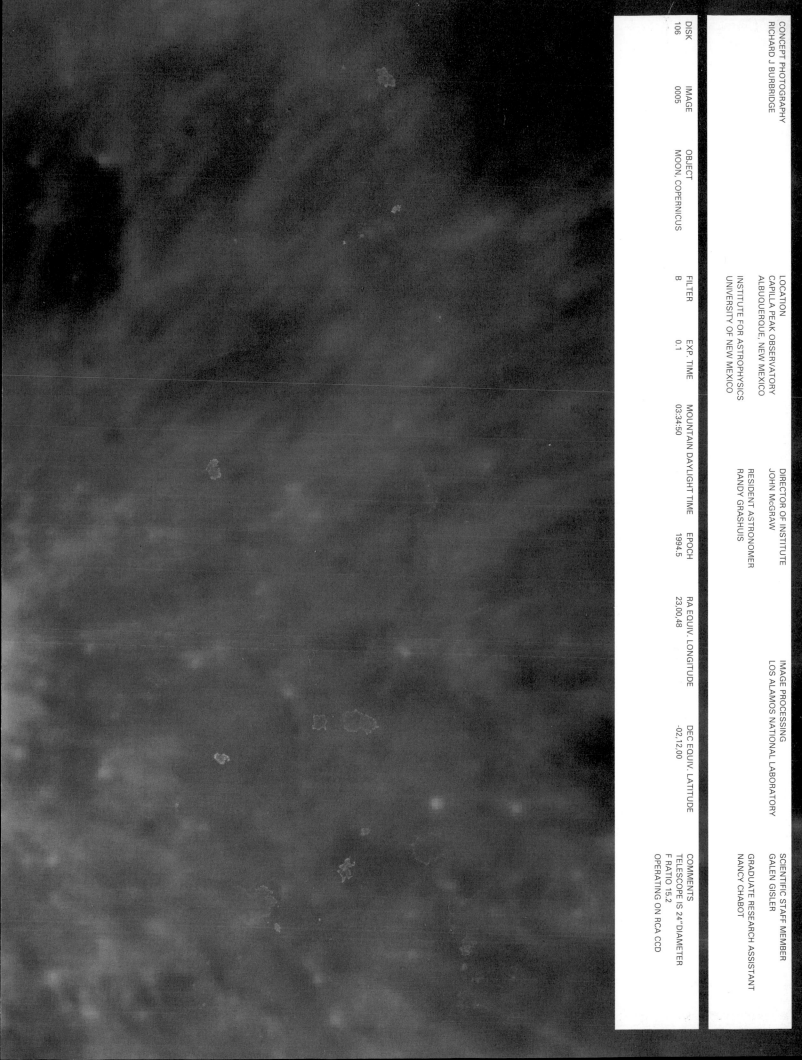

CONCEPT PHOTOGRAPHY
RICHARD J BURBRIDGE

LOCATION
CAPILLA PEAK OBSERVATORY
ALBUQUERQUE, NEW MEXICO

DIRECTOR OF INSTITUTE
JOHN McGRAW

IMAGE PROCESSING
LOS ALAMOS NATIONAL LABORATORY

SCIENTIFIC STAFF MEMBER
GALEN GISLER

INSTITUTE FOR ASTROPHYSICS
UNIVERSITY OF NEW MEXICO

RESIDENT ASTRONOMER
RANDY GRASHUIS

GRADUATE RESEARCH ASSISTANT
NANCY CHABOT

DISK	IMAGE	OBJECT	FILTER	EXP. TIME	MOUNTAIN DAYLIGHT TIME	EPOCH	RA EQUIV. LONGITUDE	DEC EQUIV. LATITUDE	COMMENTS
106	0005	MOON, COPERNICUS	B	0.1	03:34:50	1994.5	23,00,48	-02,12,00	TELESCOPE IS 24"DIAMETER F RATIO 15.2 OPERATING ON RCA CCD

FIRST PUBLISHED BY BOOTH-CLIBBORN
EDITIONS, 12 PERCY STREET, LONDON W1P 9FE
©1995

DESIGN
SEAN PERKINS, KATE TREGONING

CONCEPT PHOTOGRAPHY
RICHARD J BURBRIDGE

TEXT
SEAN PERKINS, RALPH ARDILL, ADRIAN CADDY,
IN ASSOCIATION WITH IMAGINATION LTD

EDITED AND COMPILED BY
SEAN PERKINS

ISBN 1 873968 20 5

ACKNOWLEDGMENTS: THIS BOOK WOULD NOT HAVE BEEN POSSIBLE WITHOUT THE CONTRIBUTION AND CONTINUING SUPPORT OF GARY WITHERS, MANAGING AND CREATIVE DIRECTOR AND RALPH ARDILL, MARKETING DIRECTOR OF IMAGINATION LTD

DESIGN ASSISTANCE: MALCOLM GOLDIE, BRYAN EDMONDSON, PAUL WINTER
RESEARCH ASSISTANCE: SANDY GRICE

CAPTIONS AND ARTWORK IN THIS BOOK ARE BASED ON MATERIAL SUPPLIED BY THE ENTRANTS. WHILE EVERY EFFORT HAS BEEN MADE TO ENSURE THEIR ACCURACY, BOOTH-CLIBBORN EDITIONS DOES NOT UNDER ANY CIRCUMSTANCES ACCEPT ANY RESPONSIBILITY FOR ERRORS OR OMISSIONS

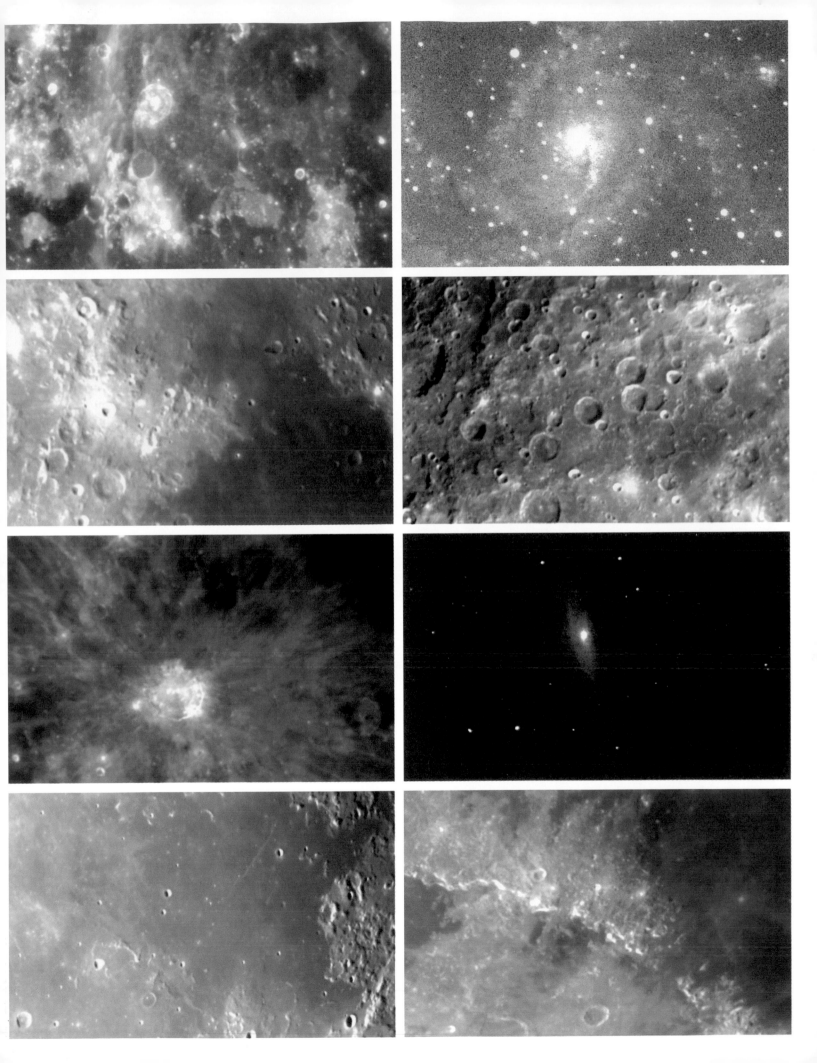

DISK 139

IMAGE 0026

OBJECT NGL 6946

FILTER R

EXP. TIME 120

MOUNTAIN DAYLIGHT TIME 05:15:52

EPOCH 1995.5

RA EQUIV. LONGITUDE 20.33.49.6

DEC EQUIV. LATITUDE 59.58.50

COMMENTS BEAUTIFUL FACE-ON SPIRAL

EXPERIENCE

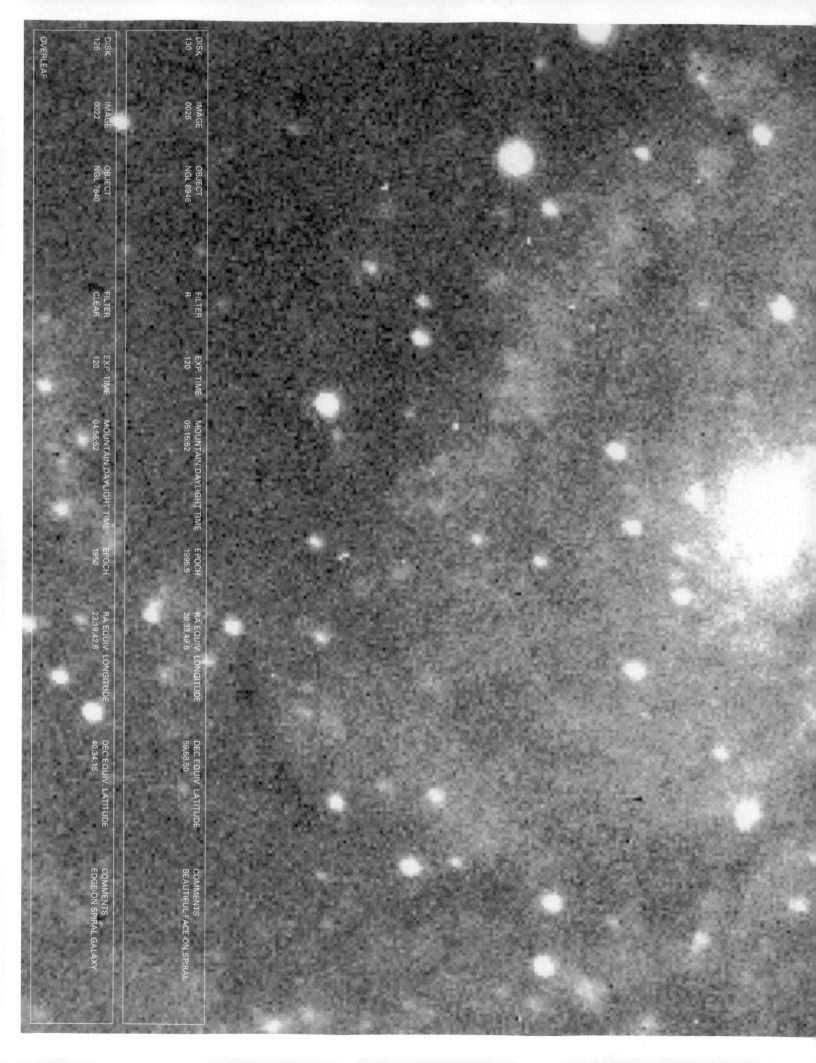

DISK 130
IMAGE 0026
OBJECT NGL 6946
FILTER R
EXP. TIME 120
MOUNTAIN DAYLIGHT TIME 05:15:52
EPOCH 1995.5
RA EQUIV. LONGITUDE 20.33.49.6
DEC EQUIV. LATITUDE 59.58.50
COMMENTS BEAUTIFUL FACE-ON SPIRAL

DISK 126
IMAGE 0022
OBJECT NGL 7640
FILTER CLEAR
EXP. TIME 120
MOUNTAIN DAYLIGHT TIME 04:56:52
EPOCH 1950
RA EQUIV. LONGITUDE 23.19.42.6
DEC EQUIV. LATITUDE 40.34.15
COMMENTS EDGE-ON SPIRAL GALAXY

OVERLEAF

'EXPERIENCE IS NOT WHAT HAPPENS TO
YOU, IT IS WHAT YOU MAKE OF WHAT
HAPPENS TO YOU.'

ALDOUS HUXLEY

'EXPERIENCE IS NOT WHAT HAPPENS TO
YOU, IT IS WHAT YOU MAKE OF WHAT
HAPPENS TO YOU.'

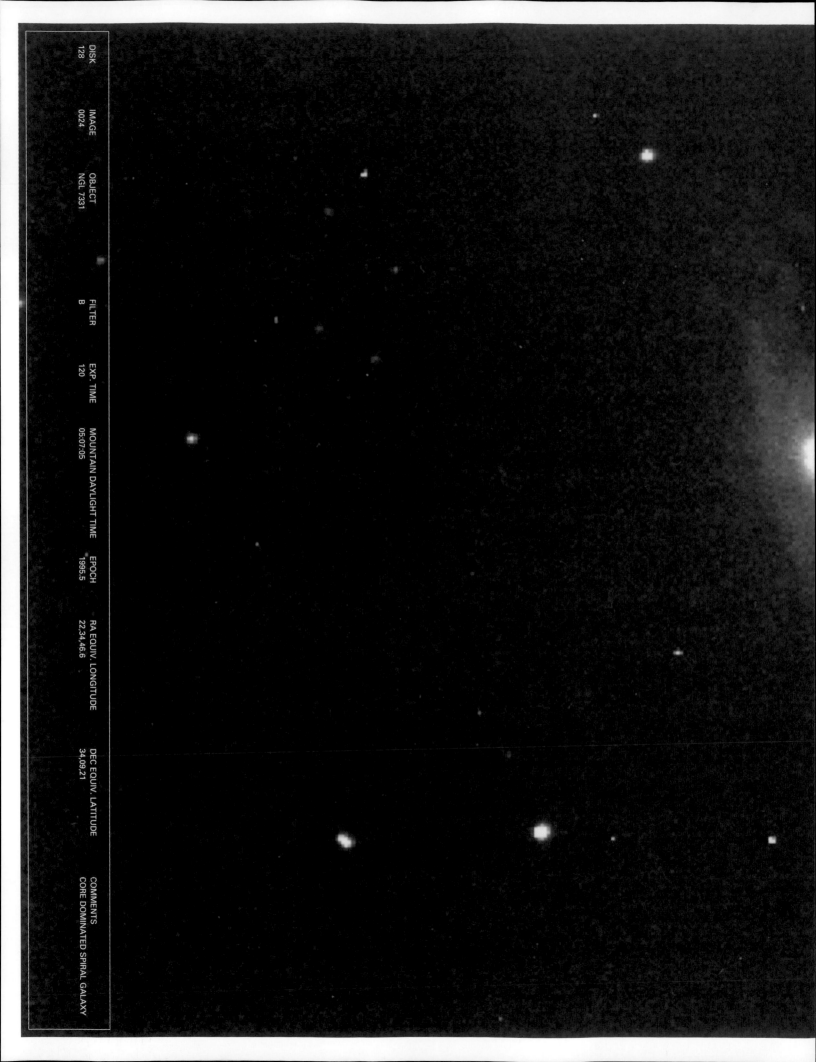

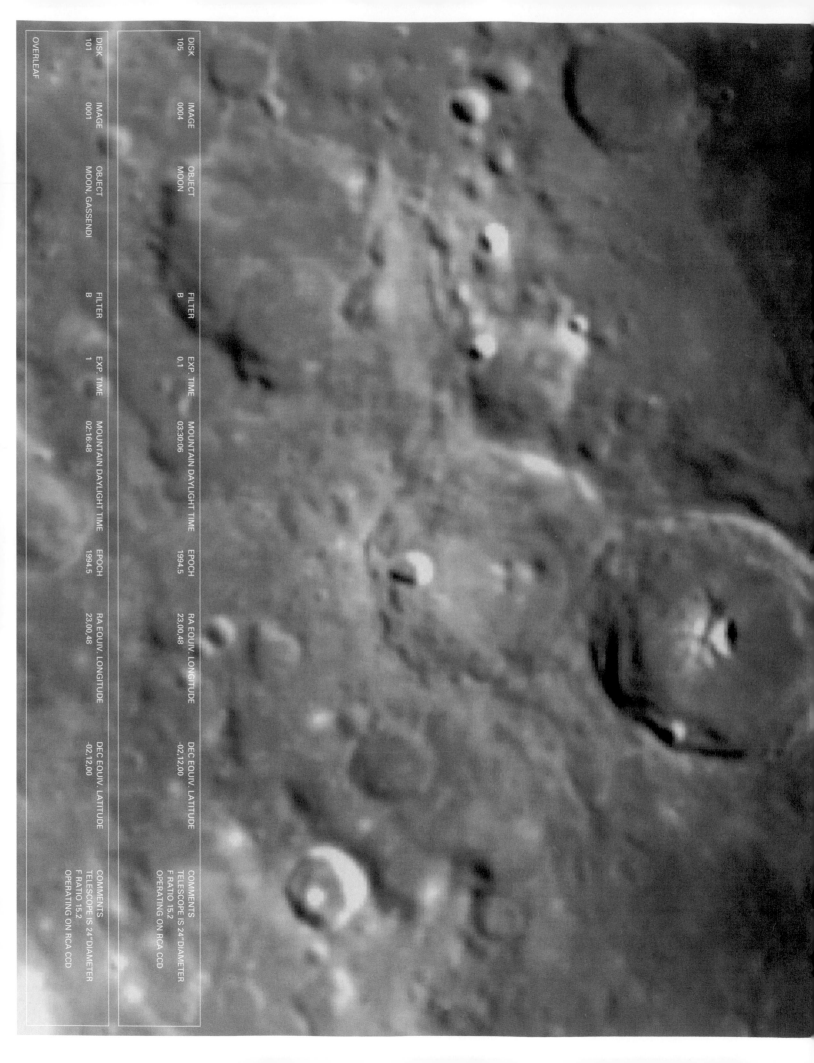

'LOOK CLOSELY AND COMPREHENSIVELY AT THESE PICTURES. INTEGRATE YOUR REACTIONS WITH ALL YOUR SPONTANEOUS RECALLS OF THE OTHER EXPERIENTIAL INFORMATION OF YOUR LIFE AS WELL AS OF OTHER LIVES AS REPORTED TO YOU. THINK AND THINK SOME MORE. FROM TIME TO TIME, HUMANS ARE ENDOWED WITH THE CAPABILITY TO DISCOVER JUST A LITTLE MORE REGARDING THE SIGNIFICANCE OF THEIR ROLE IN THE COSMIC SCENARIO. YOU TOO MIGHT CATCH ONE OF THESE 'COSMIC FISH'.'

R BUCKMINSTER FULLER

'EVERYBODY EXPERIENCES FAR MORE THAN HE UNDERSTANDS. YET IT IS EXPERIENCE, RATHER THAN UNDERSTANDING, THAT INFLUENCES BEHAVIOUR.'

MARSHALL MCLUHAN

MCLUHAN IS RIGHT. EXPERIENCE AFFECTS BEHAVIOUR. BUT AS OUR PERCEPTIONS OF THE WORLD AROUND US ARE CHALLENGED AND EVOLVE WE MUST CONTINUALLY ASK:

WHAT SHOULD THESE EXPERIENCES BE?

'YOU SEE THINGS; AND YOU SAY 'WHY?' BUT I DREAM THINGS THAT NEVER WERE; AND I SAY 'WHY NOT?'

GEORGE BERNARD SHAW

EXPERIENCE EXPLORES THIS QUESTION IN THE FORM OF A VISUAL JOURNEY.

ITS ORIGIN – THE CROSS-ROADS OF OPPORTUNITY CREATED BY THE GLOBAL COLLISION OF MARKETS, MEDIA, CULTURE AND TECHNOLOGY.

ITS DESTINATION – THE IDEAS OF THOSE WHO LIVE ON THE EDGE, RELISH NEW CHALLENGES AND RENOUNCE CONVENTIONAL THINKING.

ITS PURPOSE – TO INSPIRE YOU AND IMPRESS UPON YOU A SENSE OF ADVENTURE, EMPOWERMENT AND POSSIBILITY.

'WE KNOW WHAT HAPPENS TO PEOPLE WHO STAY IN THE MIDDLE OF THE ROAD. THEY GET RUN OVER.'

ANEURIN BEVAN

WE ANTICIPATE VIRTUAL SHOPPING MALLS AND DIGITAL SUPERHIGHWAYS.

WE HAVE MORE PRODUCTS AND LESS DIFFERENCE, MORE INFORMATION AND LESS TIME.

WE DEBATE THAT CONVENTIONAL COMMUNICATION IS NO LONGER THE ANSWER.

WE FEEL THAT EXPRESSION THROUGH NEW EXPERIENCE IS.

'ONE EYE SEES, THE OTHER FEELS.'

PAUL KLEE

WHERE THE CURRENT DEBATE ENDS THIS BOOK BEGINS.

EXPERIENCE GOES BEYOND THE RHETORIC TO VISUALLY EXPLORE THE POTENTIAL TO DEFINE AND CREATE NEW COMMUNICATION EXPERIENCES.

IT IS A BOOK FOR THE COMMISSIONER, CREATIVE AND CONSUMER IN ALL OF US.

IT IS A BOOK ABOUT DESIGN, MEDIA, MARKETING AND ART.

IT IS A BOOK ABOUT WHATEVER YOUR BUSINESS OR OUR BUSINESS MIGHT BE(COME).

IT IS A BOOK OF IDEAS.

'AS LONG AS ONLY THE IMAGE OF THE IDEA IS PERCEIVED AND NOT ITS SUBSTANCE IT CANNOT BECOME A DRIVING FORCE – THE IDEA HAS TO TAKE SHAPE.'

PIERRE DE COUBERTIN

EACH IDEA COMMUNICATES TO OUR SENSES ON A MULTITUDE OF LEVELS.

IN A MOMENT, LIFETIME OR SOMEWHERE IN BETWEEN.

EACH CHALLENGES THE BOUNDARIES OF CONVENTION TO REDEFINE AND ENLIGHTEN.

ALL UNITED BY THE INSIGHT AND IMAGINATION OF THEIR CREATORS AND THE INTEGRITY AND STYLE OF THEIR EXECUTION.

'TO ME STYLE IS JUST THE OUTSIDE OF CONTENT, AND CONTENT THE INSIDE OF STYLE. LIKE THE OUTSIDE AND THE INSIDE OF THE HUMAN BODY – BOTH GO TOGETHER, THEY CAN'T BE SEPARATED.'

JEAN-LUC GODARD

LET THESE IDEAS SHOCK, CONFUSE,
ENTERTAIN AND INSPIRE YOU.

THEY PROVIDE A VISIONARY GLIMPSE OF
A FUTURE THAT IS ALREADY AMONGST
US IF WE ARE BRAVE ENOUGH TO
PURSUE IT.

SEAN PERKINS, RALPH ARDILL,
ADRIAN CADDY. IMAGINATION LTD.

'IDEALLY A BOOK WOULD HAVE NO
ORDER TO IT AND THE READER WOULD
HAVE TO DISCOVER THEIR OWN.'

RAOUL VAN EIGEM

CLIENT
MINISTRY OF CONSTRUCTION
JAPAN

PROJECT TITLE
FOG FOREST PARK
SHOWA MEMORIAL PARK

ARCHITECT
ATSUSHI KITAGAWARA
& ILCD

PROJECT DESCRIPTION
PUBLIC PARK

FOG ARTIST
FUJIKO NAKAYA

PHOTOGRAPHY
SHIGEO OGAWA SHINKENCHIKU

P 2 AND 3

ARTIFICIAL NATURE

SEAGAIA IS A CONVENTION AND LEISURE RESORT COMPLEX ON THE SOUTHERN ISLAND OF KYUSHU, JAPAN.

THE PRINCIPAL THEME IS TO CREATE A 21ST CENTURY RESORT WHERE MAN, CULTURE AND NATURE CAN RELATE IN HARMONY.

THE OCEAN DOME IS THE RESORT'S PRINCIPLE ATTRACTION AND IS THE WORLD'S LARGEST ALL-WEATHER INDOOR WATER PARK.

CLIENT	PROJECT TITLE	PROJECT DESCRIPTION
PHOENIX RESORT LTD	OCEAN DOME, SEAGIA RESORT, JAPAN 1994	TOTAL LAND AREA 84 622M^2
		BUILDING AREA 36 291M^2
		FLOOR AREA 54 795M^2
		BEACH AREA 2 800M^2
		OCEAN AREA 6 700M^2
P 6 AND 7 (4 AND 5 PREVIOUS)		ROOF OPENING 18 000M^2

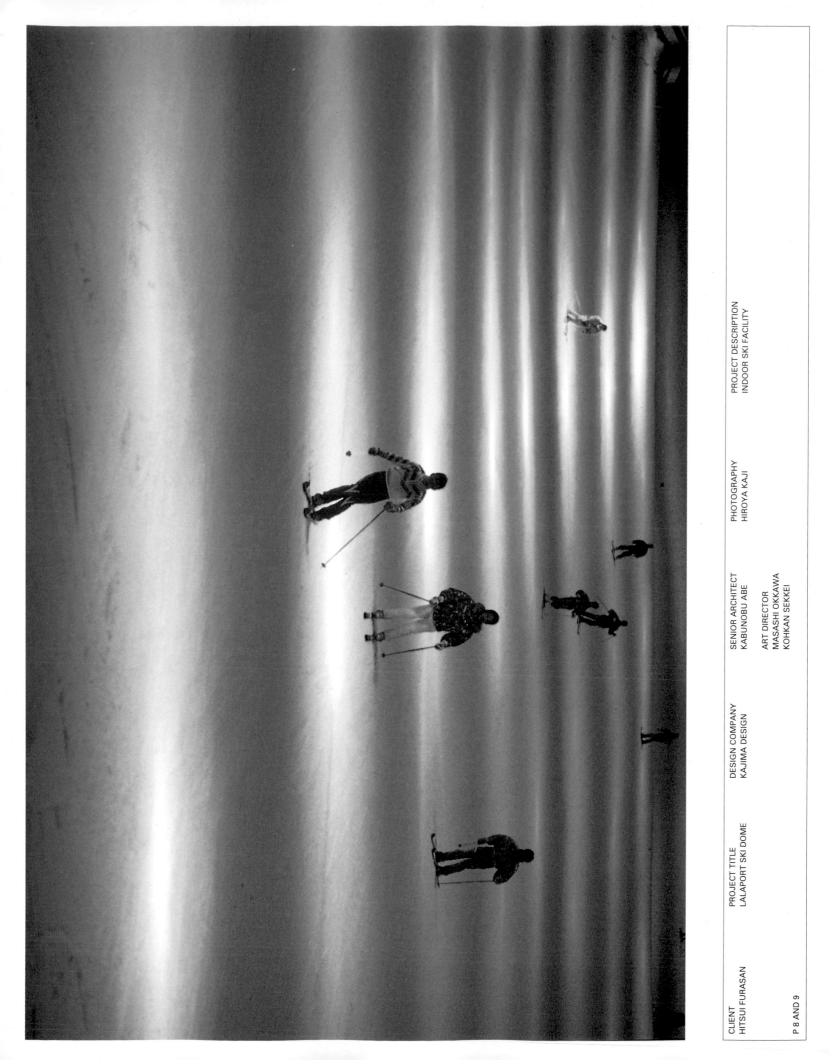

CLIENT
HITSUI FURASAN

PROJECT TITLE
LALAPORT SKI DOME

DESIGN COMPANY
KAJIMA DESIGN

SENIOR ARCHITECT
KABUNOBU ABE

ART DIRECTOR
MASASHI OKKAWA
KOHKAN SEKKEI

PHOTOGRAPHY
HIROYA KAJI

PROJECT DESCRIPTION
INDOOR SKI FACILITY

P 8 AND 9

AURAL OASIS

BAREFOOT OASIS

CLIENT	PROJECT TITLE	ARCHITECT	PROJECT DESCRIPTION
SUGINAMI-KU	SHIRU-KU ROAD POCKET PARK	KIJO ROKKAKU ARCHITECT AND ASSOCIATES	SENSORY PARK

SPONSOR
DAIKYO CO LTD

CURATORS
JOHN THACKARA
RIICHI MIYAKE

ARCHITECTS
HIROMI FUJII
KEIICHI IRIE
TOYO ITO
YUTAKA SAITO
SHIN TAKAMATSU

CAPTIONS
1 WOMB
2, 3 LASER FOREST

PROJECT TITLE
T-ZONE
A FOUR-DIMENSIONAL
EXHIBITION

EXHIBITION GRAPHICS
WHY NOT ASSOCIATES
DAVID ELLIS
ANDREW ALTMANN

EXHIBITION DESIGNER
ANDREW McKINLEY BAYLIS

CAPTIONS
1 EXHIBITS THAT RESPOND TO SOUND
2, 3 EXHIBITION INVITES
1, 4, 5, 6 PROJECTION AND VIDEO

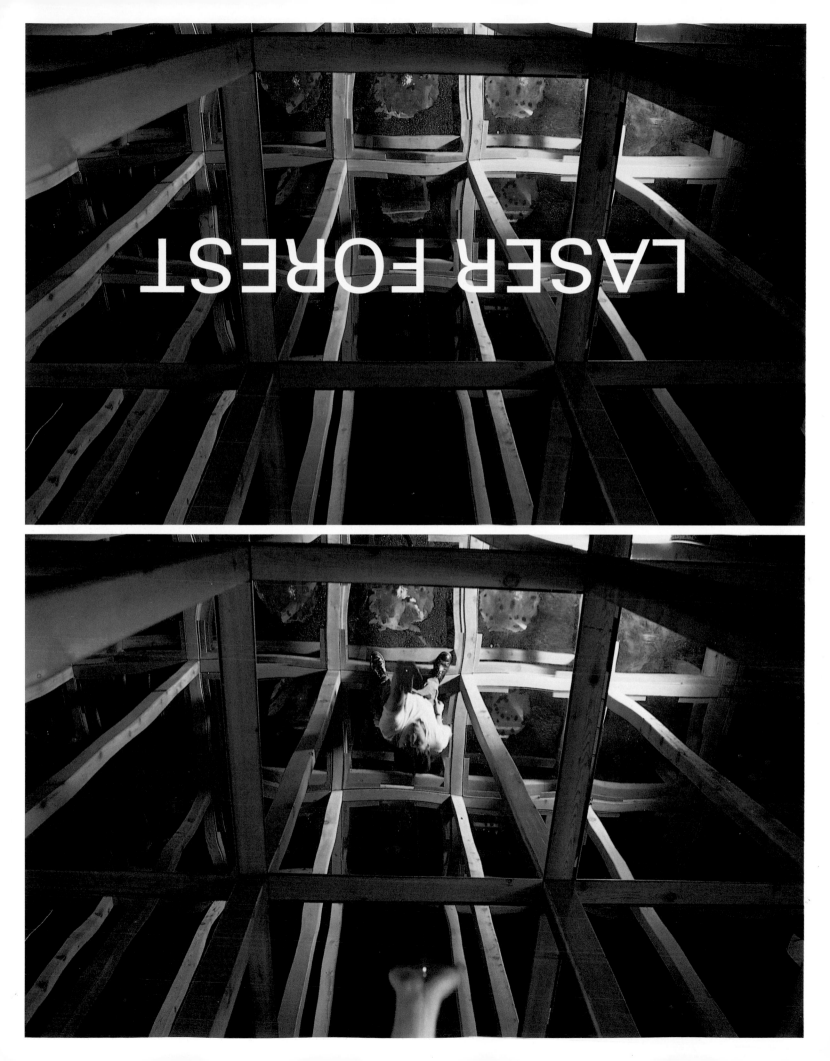

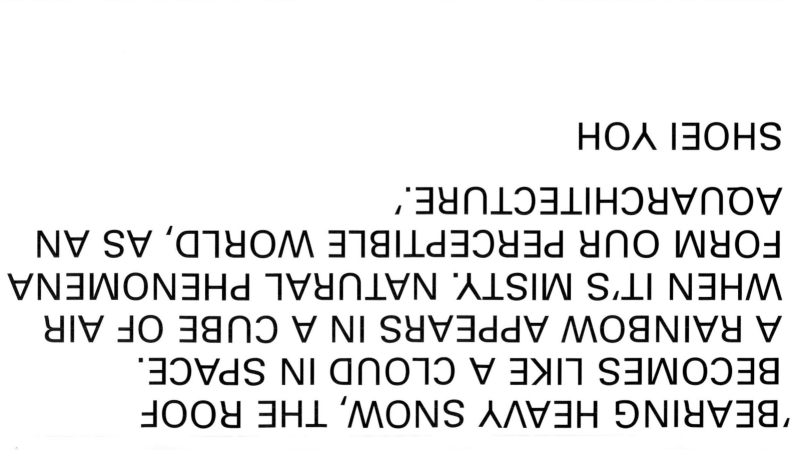

CLIENT	PROJECT TITLE	ARCHITECT	PROJECT DESCRIPTION
TOYAMA PREFECTURE	PROSPECTA '92	SHOEI YOH AND ARCHITECTS	AN OBSERVATION TOWER WITH FOG AND RAINBOW MAKING APPARATUS, DESIGNED FOR THE PURE APPRECIATION OF NATURAL PHENOMENA AND THE BEAUTIFUL LANDSCAPE. TEMPORARILY THE STRUCTURE SERVES AS AN EXPOSITION PAVILION. MORE PERMANENTLY IT SERVES AS AN EXAMPLE OF HOW ARCHITECTURE CAN BE ENDOWED WITH LIFE

'BEARING HEAVY SNOW, THE ROOF BECOMES LIKE A CLOUD IN SPACE. A RAINBOW APPEARS IN A CUBE OF AIR WHEN IT'S MISTY, NATURAL PHENOMENA FORM OUR PERCEPTIBLE WORLD, AS AN AQUARCHITECTURE.'

SHOEI YOH

ARTIST
CHRISTO

P 18

CAPTIONS
1
2
3
4

PROJECT TITLE
1, 2 VALLEY CURTAIN

PHOTOGRAPHY
HARRY SHUNK
COPYRIGHT CHRISTO 1972

PROJECT DESCRIPTION
RIFLE, COLORADO, USA 1970 – 1972
WIDTH 1250 –1368 FT; HEIGHT 185 – 365 FT
200,000 SQ FT OF NYLON POLYAMIDE
110,000 LBS OF STEEL CABLES; 800 TONS OF CONCRETE

ARTIST
CHRISTO

3, 4 PROJECT TITLE
THE UMBRELLAS

PHOTOGRAPHY
WOLFGANG VOLZ
COPYRIGHT CHRISTO 1991

PROJECT DESCRIPTION
JAPAN – USA 1984 – 1991
1340 BLUE UMBRELLAS IN IBARAKI, JAPAN
HEIGHT 9 FT 8 IN; DIAMETER 28 FT 6 IN

P 19

18 FT HIGH
24 MILES LONG
2 MILLION SQ FT OF NYLON FABRIC
90 MILES OF STEEL CABLE
2050 STEEL POLES

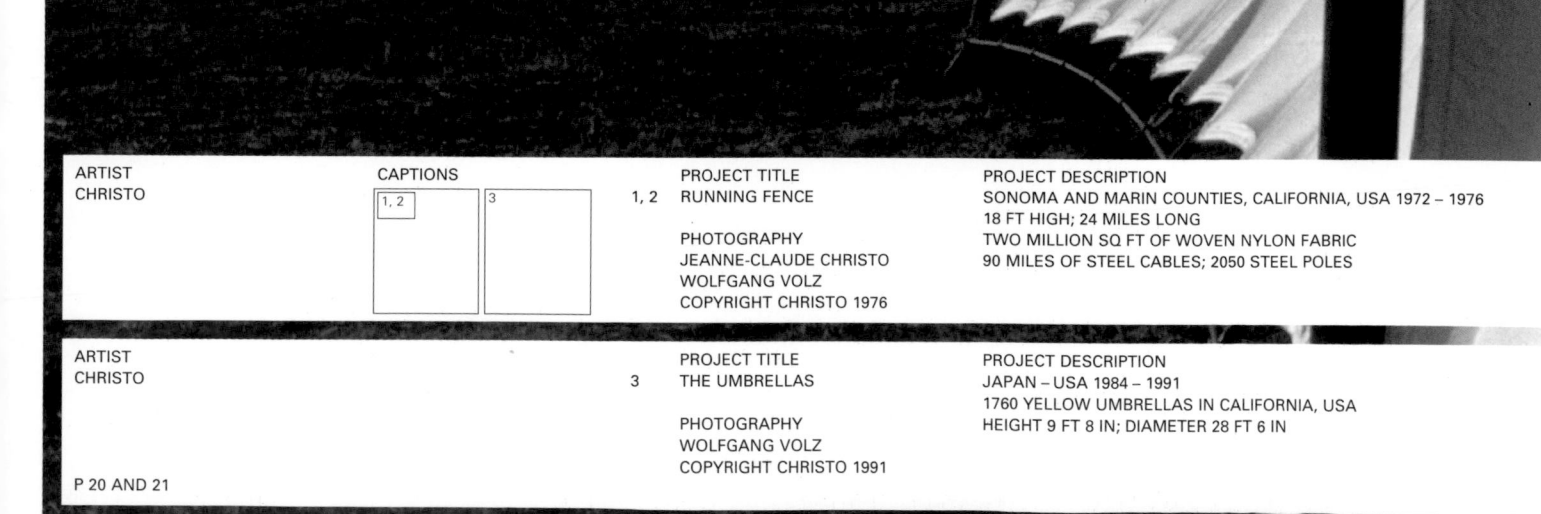

ARTIST	CAPTIONS			PROJECT TITLE	PROJECT DESCRIPTION
CHRISTO	1, 2	3	1, 2	RUNNING FENCE	SONOMA AND MARIN COUNTIES, CALIFORNIA, USA 1972 – 1976
					18 FT HIGH; 24 MILES LONG
				PHOTOGRAPHY	TWO MILLION SQ FT OF WOVEN NYLON FABRIC
				JEANNE-CLAUDE CHRISTO	90 MILES OF STEEL CABLES; 2050 STEEL POLES
				WOLFGANG VOLZ	
				COPYRIGHT CHRISTO 1976	

ARTIST		PROJECT TITLE	PROJECT DESCRIPTION
CHRISTO	3	THE UMBRELLAS	JAPAN – USA 1984 – 1991
			1760 YELLOW UMBRELLAS IN CALIFORNIA, USA
		PHOTOGRAPHY	HEIGHT 9 FT 8 IN; DIAMETER 28 FT 6 IN
		WOLFGANG VOLZ	
		COPYRIGHT CHRISTO 1991	

CLIENT
CABLE & WIRELESS

EXPOSURE
GLOBAL TV

P 22 AND 23 (24 AND 25, 26 AND 27, 28 AND 29 OVERLEAF)

PROJECT TITLE
THE LINE

PHOTOGRAPHY
KEVIN GRIFFIN

SCULPTOR
JONATHON FROUD

CREATIVES
DAVE BUONAGUIDI
NARESH RAMCHANDANI

ADVERTISING AGENCY
CHIAT DAY

PROJECT DESCRIPTION
AN ENVIRONMENTAL LANDART PROJECT TO PROMOTE CABLE & WIRELESS'
GLOBAL DIGITAL HIGHWAY

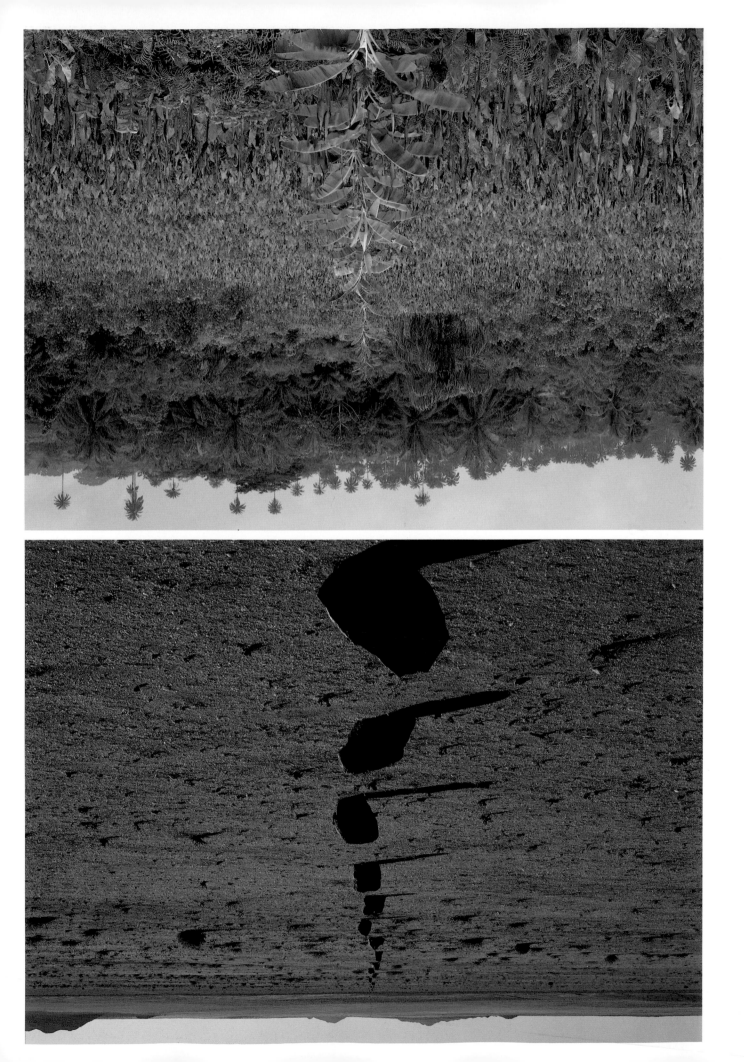

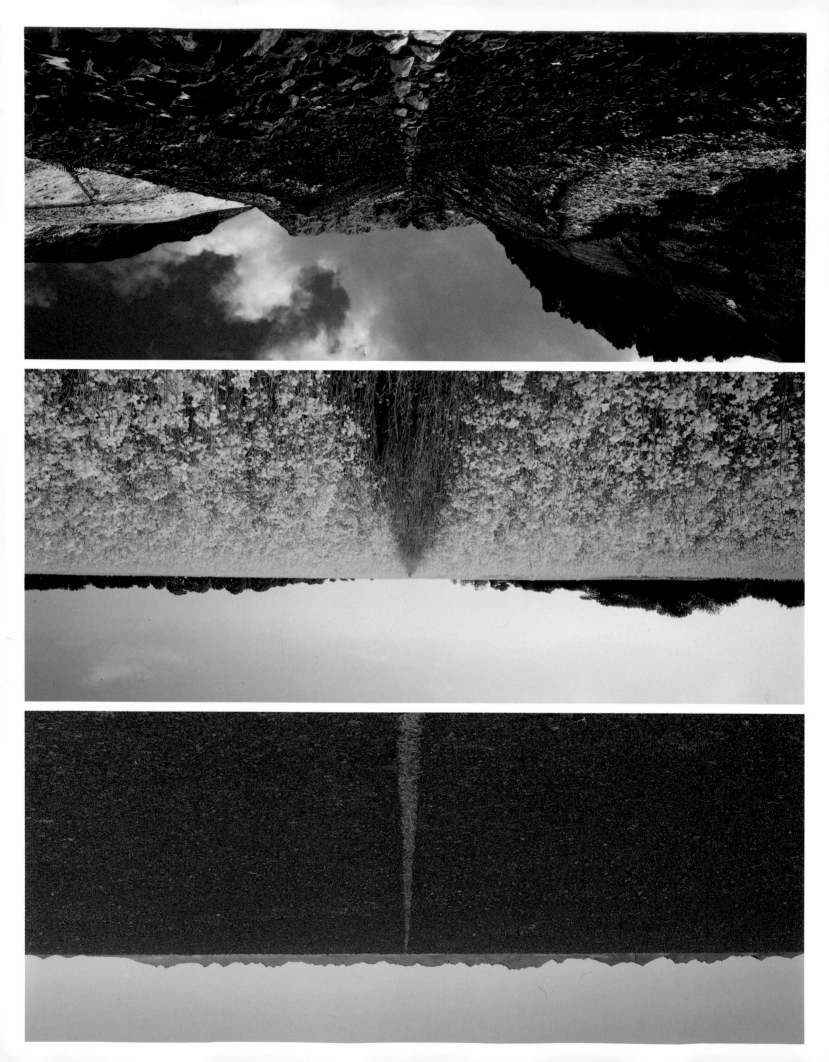

'WE ARE SHOWN THE PATH TAKEN BY THE COMPANY'S CABLE THROUGH SOME INSPIRATIONAL PARTS OF THE WORLD.'

CABLE & WIRELESS

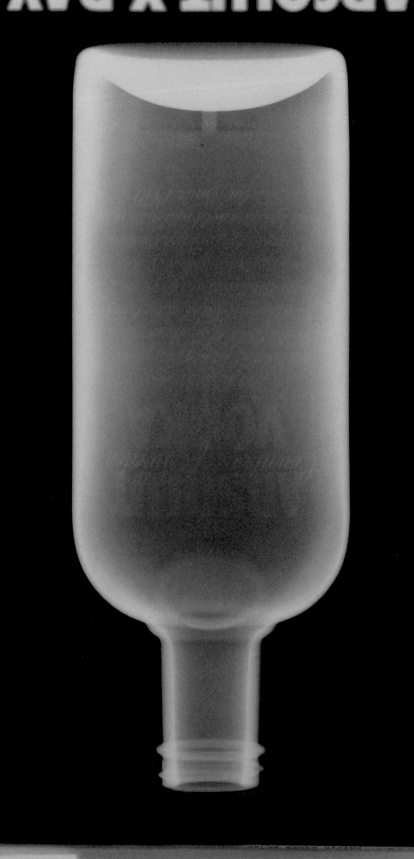

ABSOLUT X-RAY.

CLEARLY THERE IS NO PURER VODKA THAN ABSOLUT. DO IT JUSTICE DRINK IT NEAT AT 0°C.

CLIENT
ABSOLUT VODKA

ADVERTISING AGENCY
TBWA

CREATIVES
TREVOR BEATTIE
STEVE CHETHAM
NIGEL ROSE

P 30 AND 31

CAPTIONS
1
2

PROJECT DESCRIPTION
1   ABSOLUT X-RAY, ADVERTISEMENT 1993
2   ABSOLUT SPRING, 48 SHEET POSTER 1994

CLIENT
OKAWABATA CITY

PROJECT TITLE
EGG OF WINDS

ARCHITECT
TOYO ITO

PROJECT DESCRIPTION
TOWN GATE FOR OKAWABATA RIVER CITY 21, 1991

TOYO ITO

'AT THE TOWN GATE FOR OKAWABATA RIVER CITY 21, IS THE EGG OF WINDS. IT IS AN EGG 16 METRES LONG AND 8 METRES IN DIAMETER, WRAPPED WITH ALUMINIUM PANELS, FLOATING IN FRONT OF TWO HIGH-RISE BUILDINGS. DURING THE DAY THE EGG IS MERELY AN OBJECT THAT REFLECTS SUNLIGHT, BUT AT NIGHT IT DISPLAYS BOTH PRE-RECORDED VIDEO IMAGES AND TELEVISION BROADCASTS ON INTERNAL SCREENS VISIBLE THROUGH THE PARTLY PUNCHED ALUMINIUM PAN-ELED SURFACE. THE SHINY SILVER EGG OF DAYTIME AT NIGHT BECOMES A VAGUE, UNREAL 3D PRESENCE LIKE A HOLOGRAM. PASSERS-BY LOOK UP AT THE EGG, STOP FOR A MOMENT, AND THEN WALK AWAY. IT IS AN OBJECT OF VIDEO IMAGES THAT SEEM TO COME AND GO WITH THE WIND,'

'WHERE THERE IS NO VISION, THE PEOPLE PERISH.' BIBLE, HEBREW·

ARCHITECT	PROJECT TITLE	LOCATION	PHOTOGRAPHY
TADAO ANDO	CHURCH ON THE WATER	TOMAMU, HOKKAIDO JAPAN	MITSUO MATSUOKA

TADAO ANDO

'AS ONE CLIMBS UP A GENTLE SLOPE LISTENING TO THE SOUND OF THE STREAM, ONE FINDS ONESELF WITHIN THE BOX OF LIGHT. THE TOP IS OPEN, AND FOUR CROSSES ARE STANDING FACING EACH OTHER UNDER THE VAULT OF SKY. HERE ONE COMMUNICATES WITH NATURE AS ONE LISTENS TO THE SOUNDS OF WATER, WIND AND THE CHIRPING OF BIRDS. I WISHED TO BUILD AN ARCHITECTURE WHICH WOULD APPEAL NOT ONLY TO THE EYES OF VIEWERS BUT TO ALL THE FIVE SENSES OF MEN.

THE SCENERY WHICH IS CUT OUT BY THE FRAME OF THE DOOR CHANGES WITH TIME AND IS REFLECTED ON THE WATER. IN THE CHANGES ONE FEELS NATURE AND THE SACRED AT THE SAME TIME.'

ARCHITECT
TADAO ANDO

PROJECT TITLE
CHURCH OF THE LIGHT

LOCATION
IBARAGI, OSAKA
JAPAN

PHOTOGRAPHY
MITSUO MATSUOKA

CHURCH OF THE LIGHT
'FOR WE WALK BY FAITH, NOT BY SIGHT.'
BIBLE, II CORINTHIANS

BENETTON

CLIENT	PROJECT TITLE	ARCHITECT	PROJECT DESCRIPTION
BENETTON GROUP	FABRICA	TADAO ANDO	THE BUILDING IS A RESEARCH CENTRE THAT ACCEPTS YOUNG PEOPLE FROM AROUND THE WORLD
	BENETTON ART SCHOOL		WITH ACHIEVEMENTS IN THE APPLIED ARTS SUCH AS ARCHITECTURE, DESIGN, PHOTOGRAPHY,
			GRAPHIC ART, THE IMAGE MEDIA AND TEXTILES, AS WELL AS IN WOODWORKING, METALWORKING AND
			CERAMICS. THE INFUSION AND ULTIMATE HARMONY OF CONTRASTING CULTURES IS AN ADDITIONAL
			THEME OF THE CENTRE, WHICH ANTICIPATES AND PROMOTES ACTIVE EXCHANGE AMONG THE YOUNG
			PEOPLE WHO GATHER THERE

'IF THE EARTH HAS BECOME A GLOBAL VILLAGE, THEN BENETTON IS THE VILLAGE CLOTHING STORE. AND, LIKE EVERY GOOD LEADING CITIZEN, IT FEELS AN OBLIGA-TION TO NOT ONLY SUCCEED IN BUSINESS BUT ALSO TO IMPROVE THE NEIGHBOUR-HOOD. ITS COMMUNICATIONS PRO-GRAMME IS MEANT TO RAISE AN AWARE-NESS OF ISSUES THAT AFFECT THE LIFE OF THE VILLAGE. ITS ADVERTISING REFLECTS ITS CONCERNS FOR THE COMMUNITY.

TO FURTHER THESE EFFORTS BENETTON HAS FOUNDED COLORS, THE VILLAGE MAGAZINE. IT IS ABOUT WHAT PEOPLE IN THE VILLAGE DO AND SEE AND THINK. IT IS ABOUT HOW EACH PERSON IN THE VILLAGE IS DIFFERENT.

IT'S A VISUAL MAGAZINE. AND BECAUSE THE PEOPLE IN THE VILLAGE SPEAK DIFFERENT LANGUAGES, COLORS APPEARS IN FIVE BILINGUAL EDITIONS.'

TIBOR KALMAN

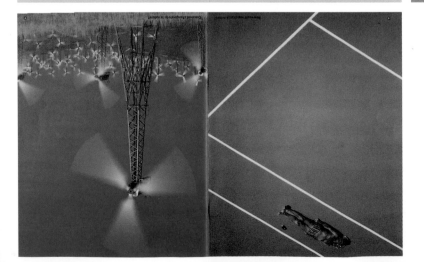

P 40 AND 41 (42 AND 43 OVERLEAF)

CLIENT
BENETTON GROUP

PROJECT TITLE
COLORS MAGAZINE
NOS 6, 7 AND 8

PRINT RUN
1 MILLION COPIES

DESIGNER
TIBOR KALMAN

EDITORS
OLIVIERO TOSCANI
TIBOR KALMAN

TIBOR KALMAN

PROJECT DESCRIPTION
'COLORS, WHICH IS PUBLISHED BY BENETTON, IS NOT A CATALOGUE IN DISGUISE, OR AN ADVERTORIAL. IT'S A REAL MAGAZINE THAT TAKES ITS GLOBAL OUTLOOK AND ITS UNDERLYING EDITORIAL MESSAGE – DIVERSITY IS GOOD – FROM BENETTON'S WELL KNOWN ADVERTISING CAMPAIGN.'

'THE MESSAGE OF THIS MAGAZINE IS THAT YOUR CULTURE (WHOEVER YOU ARE) IS AS IMPORTANT AS OUR CULTURE (WHOEVER WE ARE).'

TIBOR KALMAN

'DEREK JARMAN WAS ONE OF ENGLAND'S MOST ADMIRED FILMMAKERS. HE WAS ALSO AN ACTOR, A WRITER, A PAINTER, A SET DESIGNER AND AN OUTSPOKEN CAMPAIGNER FOR GAY RIGHTS. IN 1986 HE TESTED HIV POSITIVE.

JARMAN WROTE AND DIRECTED BLUE WHILE LOSING HIS SIGHT, A SIDE EFFECT OF AIDS.

FOR 76 MINUTES THE ONLY VISUAL IMAGE IS A BLUE SCREEN WITH AN OCCASIONAL SHADOW. AS THE AUDIENCE STARES INTO THE BLUE, THEY HEAR A SOUNDTRACK OF MUSIC, SOUNDS AND ACTOR'S VOICES READING LINES FROM JARMAN'S EVOCATIVE HOSPITAL DIARIES.

JARMAN DIED ON FEBRUARY 19 1994, AT THE AGE OF 52 AFTER FINALLY REFUSING THE MEDICINE THAT WAS KEEPING HIM ALIVE.'

COLORS ISSUE NO 7

WRITER/DIRECTOR	TITLE	SOUND DESIGN	VOICES	PRODUCERS
DEREK JARMAN	BLUE	MARVIN BLACK	JOHN QUENTIN	JAMES MACKAY
			NIGEL TERRY	TAKASHI ASAI
	COMPOSER	ASSOCIATE DIRECTOR	DEREK JARMAN	
	SIMON FISHER TURNER	DAVID LEWIS	TILDA SWINTON	A BASILISK COMMUNICATIONS/
				UPLINK PRODUCTION

P 48 AND 49 (44 AND 45, 46 AND 47 PREVIOUS)

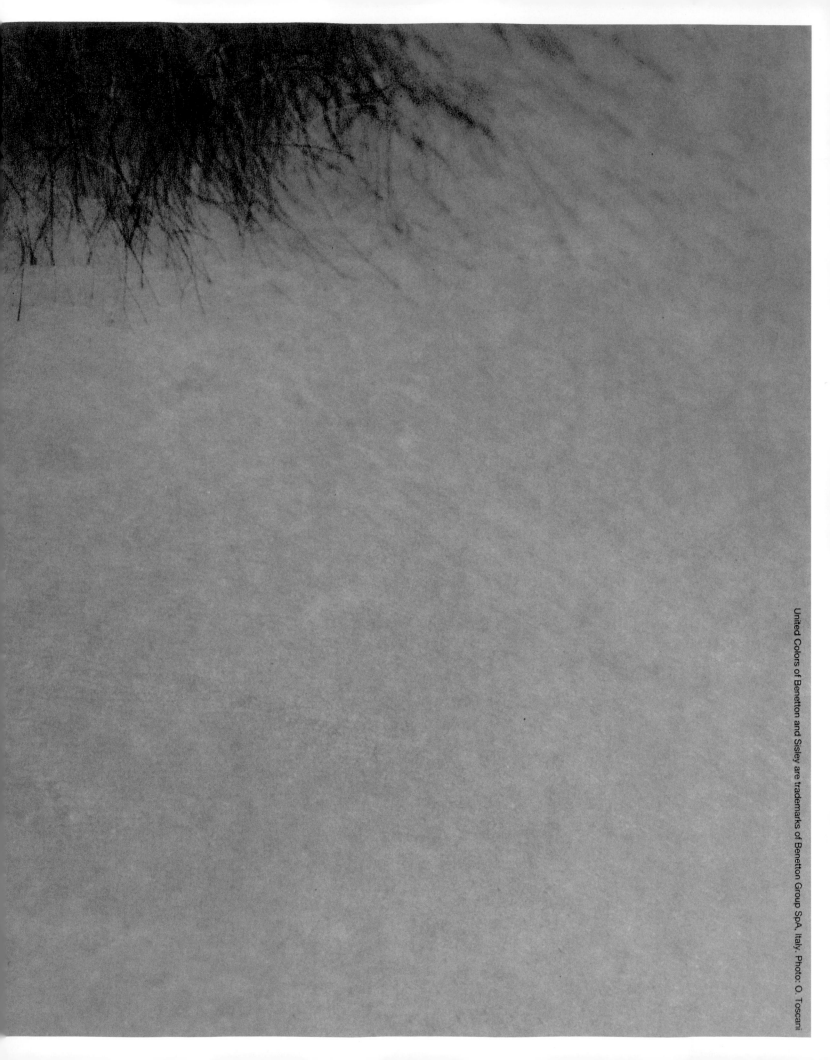

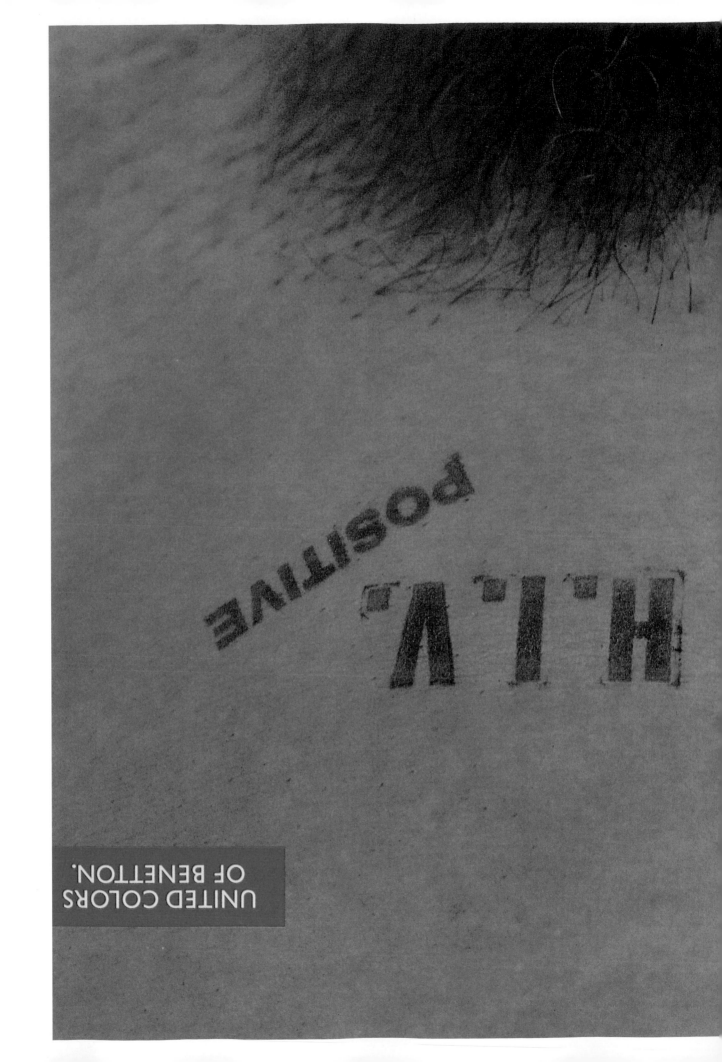

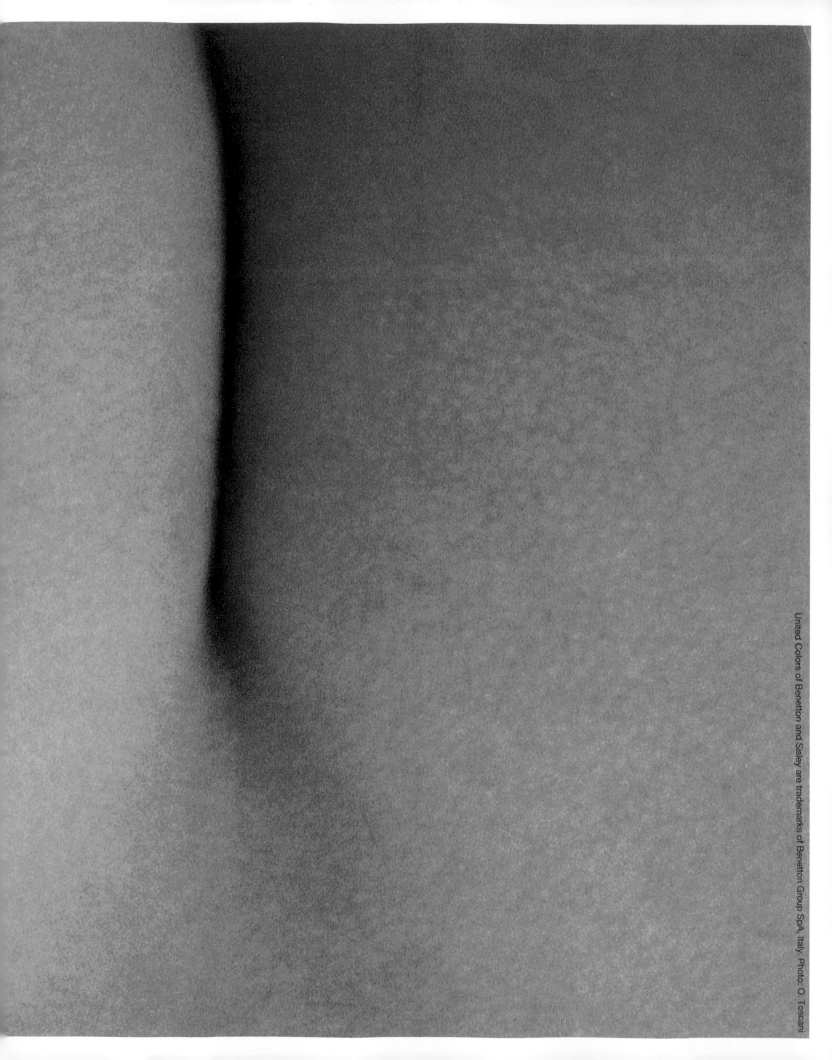

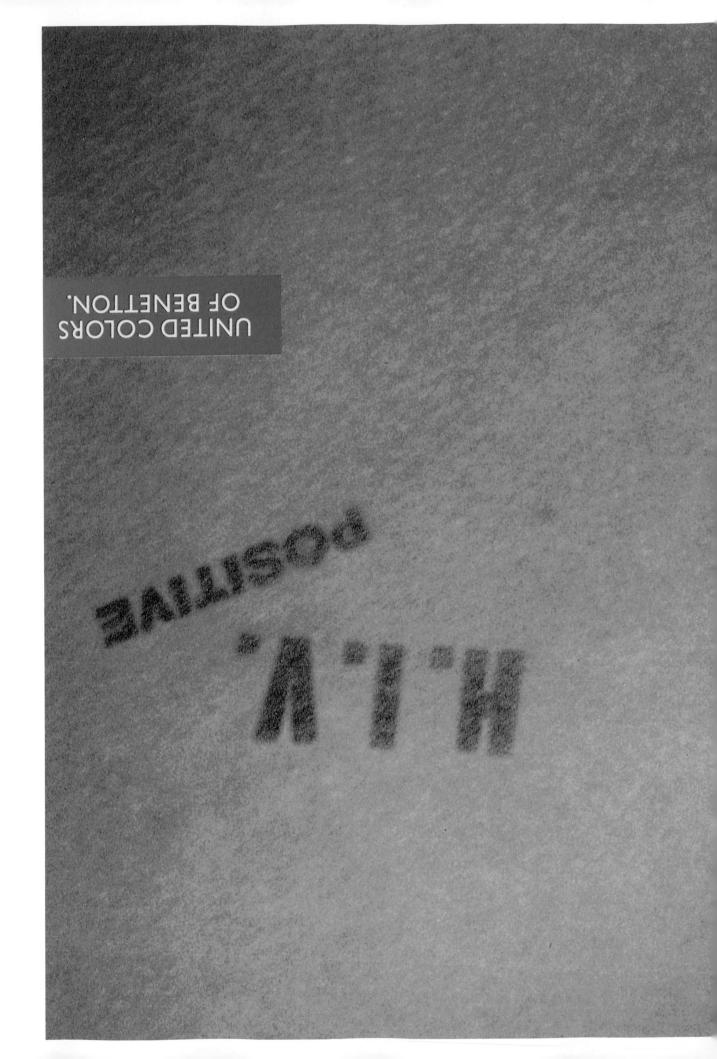

'FEW PEOPLE CAN SEE GENIUS IN
SOMEONE WHO HAS OFFENDED THEM.'

ROBERTSON DAVIES

CLIENT
BENETTON GROUP

CREATIVE DIRECTOR
OLIVIERO TOSCANI

PROJECT DESCRIPTION
BENETTON PRESS AND POSTER ADVERTISING

P 54 AND 55 (50 AND 51, 52 AND 53 PREVIOUS)

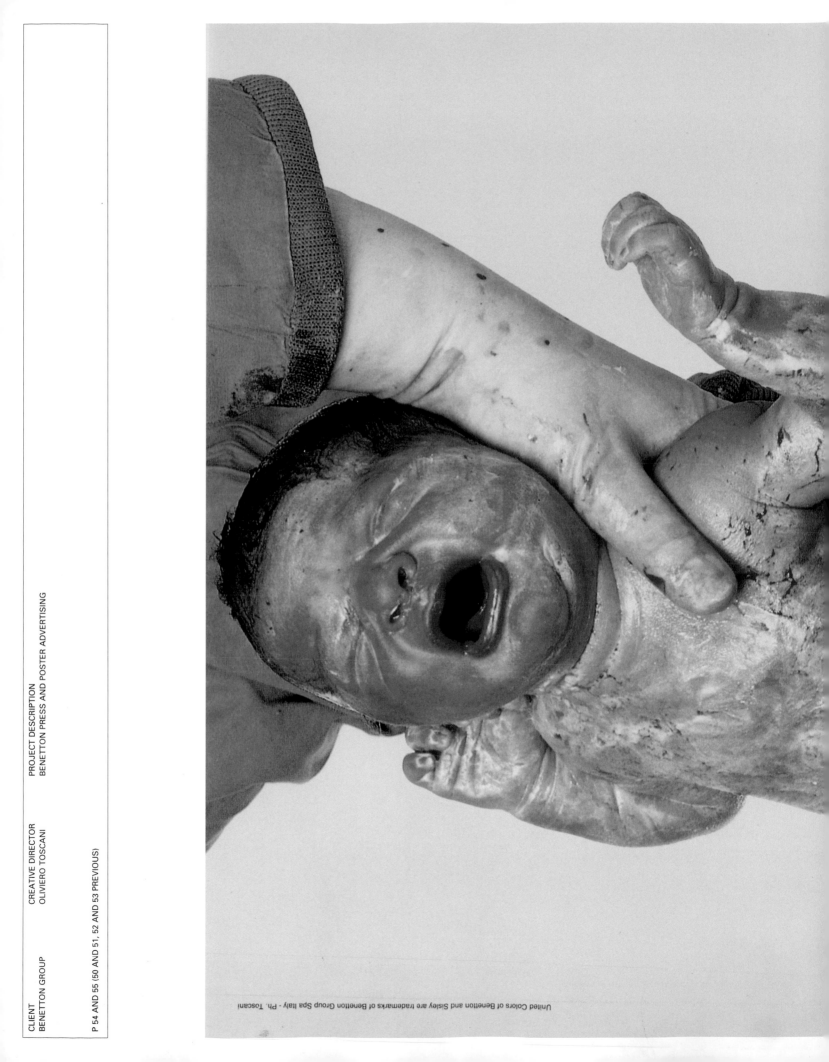

UNITED COLORS
OF BENETTON.

CLIENT
MUSEUM BOYMANS –
VAN BEUNINGEN,
ROTTERDAM

P 56 AND 57

EXHIBITION
THE PHYSICAL SELF
27 10 91 – 12 01 92

CURATOR
PETER GREENAWAY

PROJECT DESCRIPTION
THE EXHIBITION WAS MADE UP OF ITEMS AND IMAGES EXCLUSIVELY FROM
THE BOYMANS-VAN BEUNINGEN COLLECTION THAT COMMENT UPON THE
PHYSICAL HUMAN PREDICAMENT. THE PIECES WERE CHOSEN BY GUEST
CURATOR PETER GREENAWAY. EXHIBITS INCLUDED 4 UNCLOTHED FIGURES.
THESE FIGURES ARE THE TEMPLATES – THE BASIC MODELS TO WHICH ALL
THE PAINTINGS, SCULPTURES AND ARTIFACTS IN THE EXHIBITION RELATE

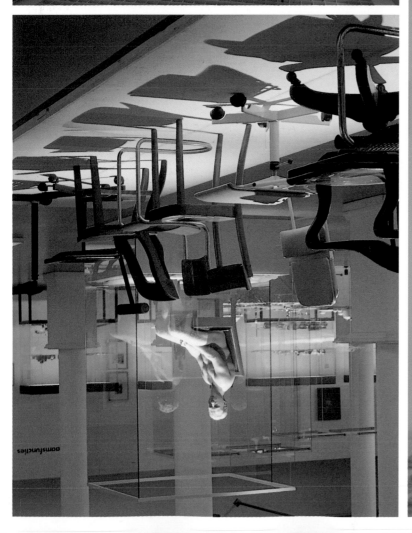

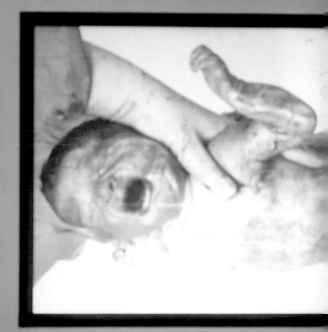

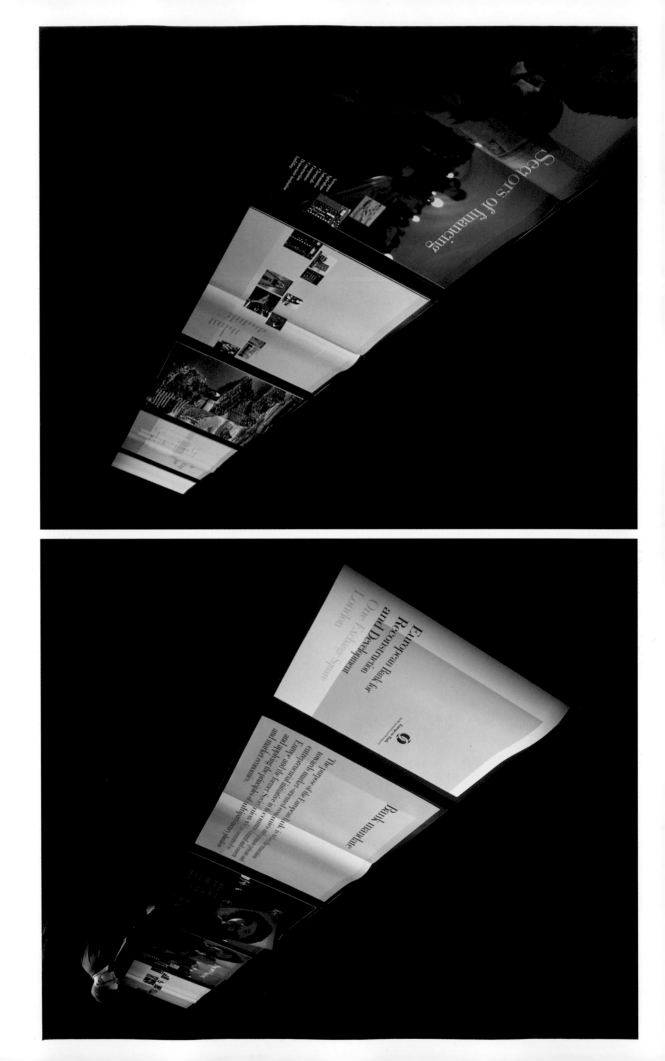

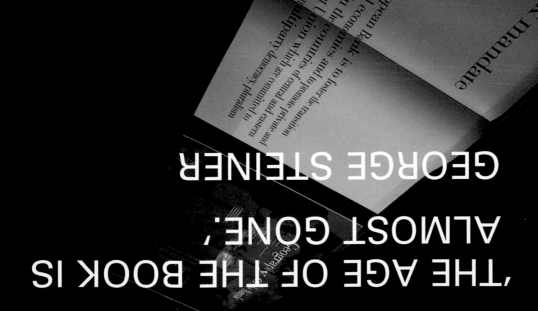

'THE AGE OF THE BOOK IS
ALMOST GONE;'
GEORGE STEINER

CLIENT
EUROPEAN BANK FOR RECONSTRUCTION
AND DEVELOPMENT

DESIGN COMPANY
WILLIAMS AND PHOA

PHOTOGRAPHY
JON PREW

INTERIOR DESIGNERS
KONU AND MORROW

PROJECT DESCRIPTION
AN EXHIBITION 'BOOK' DOCUMENTING THE EUROPEAN BANK'S INITIATIVES IN EASTERN
EUROPE

CLIENT	PROJECT TITLE	DESIGN COMPANY	PHOTOGRAPHY	PROJECT DESCRIPTION
FOREIGN AND COMMONWEALTH OFFICE	INVENTIVE SPIRIT	WHY NOT ASSOCIATES	ROCCO REDONDO	EXHIBITION, BRUSSELS 1992
		GRAPHIC DESIGNERS ANDREW ALTMANN DAVID ELLIS		

P 60 AND 61

CLIENT	PROJECT TITLE	ARCHITECT	PROJECT DESCRIPTION
OBAYASHI, TOKYO	MILLENNIUM TOWER	SIR NORMAN FOSTER AND PARTNERS	MULTI-USE TOWER FOR 50,000 INHABITANTS

'WE SHAPE OUR BUILDINGS; THEREAFTER THEY SHAPE US,'

SIR WINSTON CHURCHILL

'EXPERIENCE IS NEVER LIMITED, AND IT IS NEVER COMPLETE; IT IS AN IMMENSE SENSIBILITY, A KIND OF HUGE SPIDER-WEB OF THE FINEST SILKEN THREADS SUSPENDED IN THE CHAMBER OF CONSCIOUSNESS, AND CATCHING EVERY AIRBORNE PARTICLE IN ITS TISSUE.'

HENRY JAMES

ARCHITECT	PROJECT TITLE	PHOTOGRAPHY
SANTIAGO CALATRAVA	EL ALAMILLO BRIDGE	JOHN EDWARD LINDON
	SEVILLE 1992	NICK KANE
		COURTESY ARCAID

P 64 AND 65

OVER A THREE MONTH PERIOD ADVERTS WERE PLACED IN MAGAZINES, NEWS-PAPERS, SCHOOLS AND AN OLD PEOPLES' HOME TO COLLECT AS MANY QUESTIONS AS POSSIBLE ON ANY SUBJECT – WHETHER IMPORTANT, TRIVIAL, PERSONAL OR UNIVERSAL.

FROM BEING EARTHBOUND, CONTAINED AND ENCLOSED, THE BALOON RELEASE OF THESE QUESTIONS UTILISED THE CHAOTIC POWER OF NATURE TO PLOT OUT AN INDEPENDENT AND RANDOM INFORMATION SYSTEM.

OVER THE NEXT THREE MONTHS OVER 600 ANSWERS WERE RETURNED, FROM PLACES AS DIVERSE AS CROYDON AND MURAT IN SOUTHERN FRANCE.

ARTIST
CHRIS GROTTICK

PROJECT TITLE
METASAMATISM
BALLOON PROJECT

PROJECT DESCRIPTION
AN INFORMATION SYSTEM WHICH INCORPORATES HUMAN OPINION AND NATURE TO HIGHLIGHT THE ESSENTIAL CONNECTION BETWEEN THE TWO, SEPTEMBER 1993 – MAY 1994

P 66 AND 67

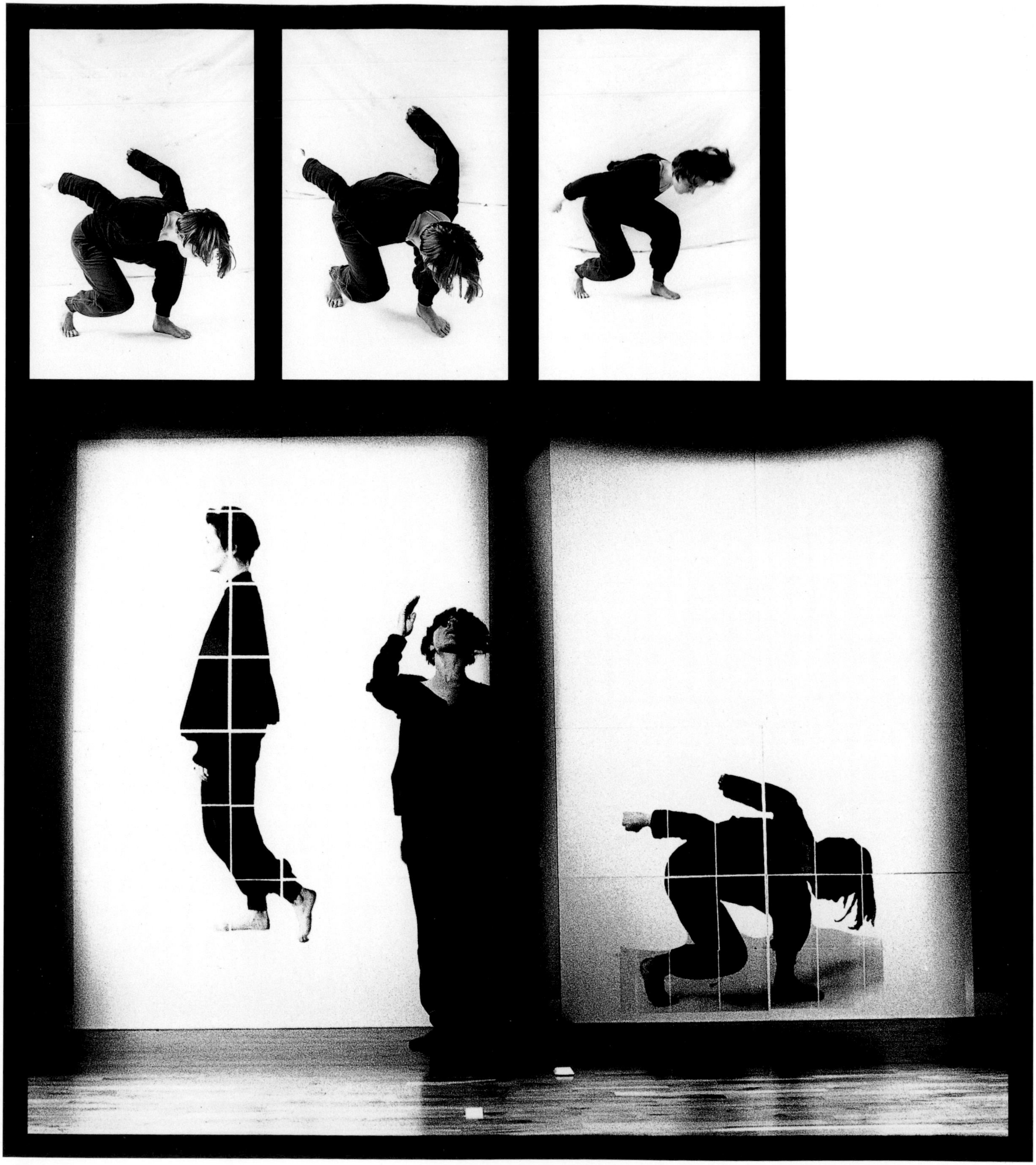

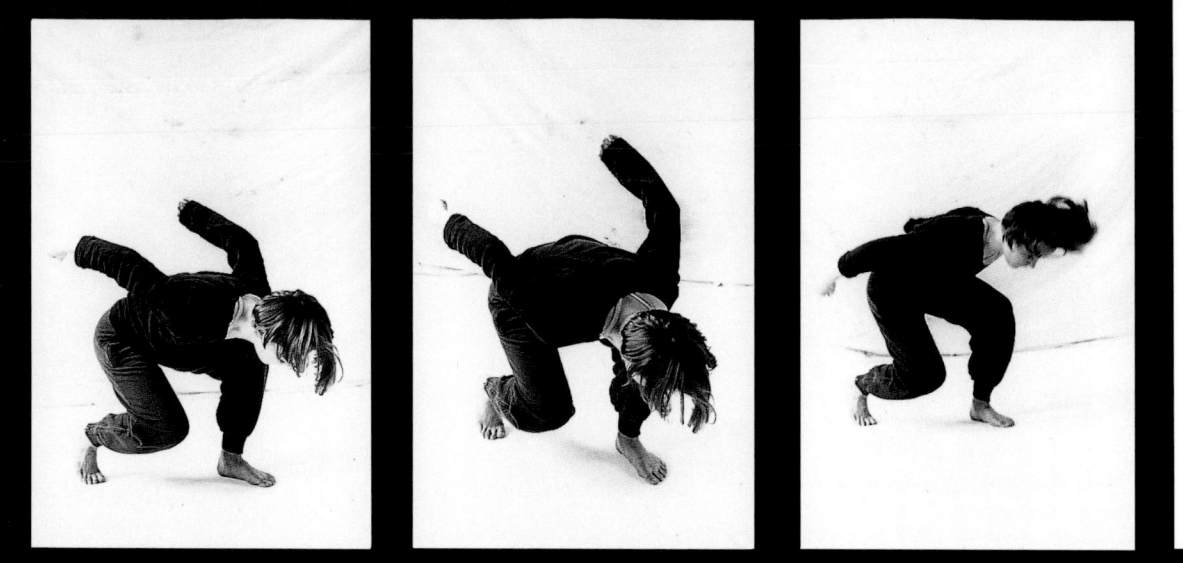

CLIENT
BARCLAYS
NEW STAGES AWARD

P 68 AND 69

PROJECT TITLE
BODY AS SITE
IMAGE AS EVENT

DANCE COMPANY
ROSEMARY BUTCHER

DANCERS
MICHAEL POPPER
MICHELLE SMITH
FIN WALKER

MUSIC
SIMON TURNER

DESIGNER
PAUL ELLIMAN

PHOTOGRAPHY
MARK LEWIS

PROJECT DESCRIPTION
LIVE INSTALLATION PERFORMANCE
1992 – 1993

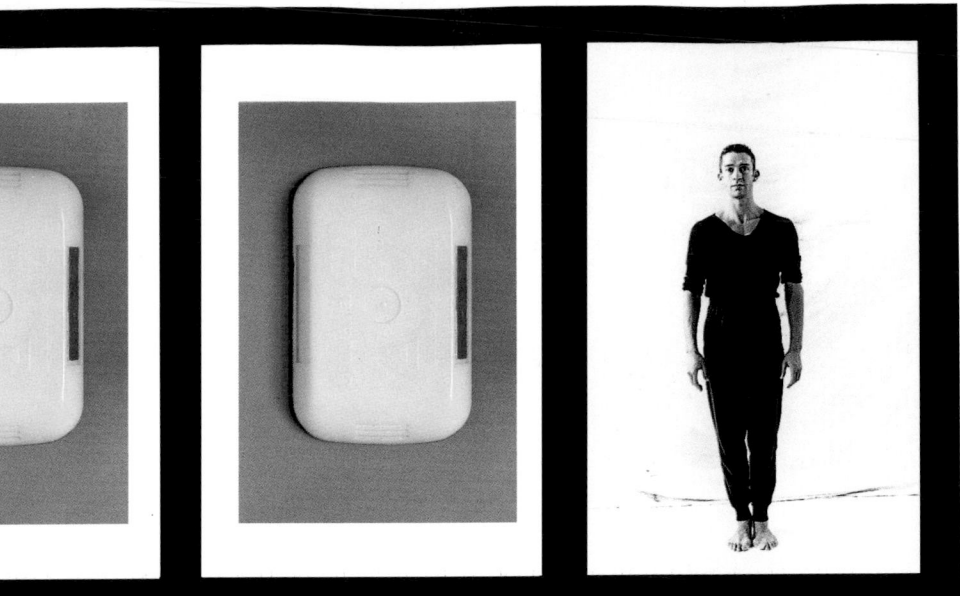

REVIEW
'THE BODY OF THE DANCER IS A POINT WHICH ARTICULATES SPACE. THE STAGE SPACE IS TRACED WITH
GEOMETRIC PATHS – CONCRETISED AS A GRIDDED MAZE IN ELLIMAN'S 'ROAD-WORK SITE' (CAT'S EYES AND
WORKING LIGHT) INSTALLATION. ECCENTRIC MIXES OF OPPOSITIONAL TENSIONS AND MOVEMENT CONTENT
CONSTRUCT THE BODY IMAGE. BUTCHER'S DANCERS CREATE A PROFOUND SENSE OF THE VOLUME OF THE STAGE
AS FEW OTHERS, EXCEPT CUNNINGHAM'S CAN.'
ANDREA PHILLIPS, HYBRID APRIL/MAY 1993

ART

ARTIST
BARBARA KRUGER

CAPTIONS

1   PROJECT DESCRIPTION
     ENAMEL/ALUMINIUM 1990 186" X 254"
     PHOTOGRAPHY DOROTHY ZIEDMAN/FREMONT
     COURTESY MARY BOONE GALLERY, NEW YORK

2   PHOTOGRAPHIC SILKSCREEN/PAPER 1990 192" X 276"
3, 4 INSTALLATIONS AT MARY BOONE GALLERY
     NEW YORK 1994 AND JANUARY 1991
2, 3, 4 PHOTOGRAPHY DOROTHY ZIEDMAN/FREMONT
     COURTESY MARY BOONE GALLERY, NEW YORK

5   INSTALLATION AT SERPENTINE GALLERY, LONDON 1994
     PHOTOGRAPHY HUGO ELENDINNING
     COURTESY SERPENTINE GALLERY, LONDON

P 72 AND 73 (70 AND 71 PREVIOUS)

The Economist

hidden agenda

NO

The Economist

Open your eyes

ADVERTISING

CLIENT
THE ECONOMIST

ADVERTISING AGENCY
SP LINTAS

TYPE AND LAYOUT DESIGN
BARBARA KRUGER

SPL WRITER/ART DIRECTOR
ADRIAN KEMSLEY

SPL TYPOGRAPHER
MARK OSBORNE

PROJECT DESCRIPTION
PAN-EUROPEAN ADVERTISING CAMPAIGN 1994

P 76 AND 77 (74 AND 75 PREVIOUS)

CAPTIONS
1 2 3

PHOTOGRAPHY
1 SANDRA LOUSADA
2 JED ROOT
3 UNKNOWN

CLIENT	PROJECT TITLE	LANGUAGE				
THE GUARDIAN NEWSPAER	THE GUARDIAN NEWSPAPER	LANGUAGE		ADVERTISING AGENCY	DESIGN COMPANY	PROJECT DESCRIPTION
				LEAGUS DELANEY	TOMATO	TV AND CINEMA ADVERTISING
						CAMPAIGN FOR THE GUARDIAN
						NEWSPAPER 1993

CREATIVES
TIM DELANEY
STEVE DUNN
CHRISTINE JONES

DIRECTOR
GRAHAM WOOD

P 78 AND P 79 (80 AND 81 OVERLEAF)

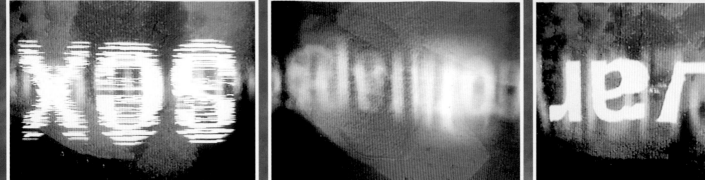

CLIENT
NEWS INTERNATIONAL

PROJECT TITLE
TODAY NEWSPAPER ADVERTISING

ADVERTISING AGENCY
BAINSFAIR SHARKEY TROTT

DESIGN COMPANY
TOMATO

PROJECT DESCRIPTION
ADVERTISING CAMPAIGN FOR
TODAY NEWSPAPER 1994

DIRECTOR
KEVIN GODLEY

CREATIVE
PAUL LEEVES

DESIGNER
GRAHAM WOOD

P 82 AND 83

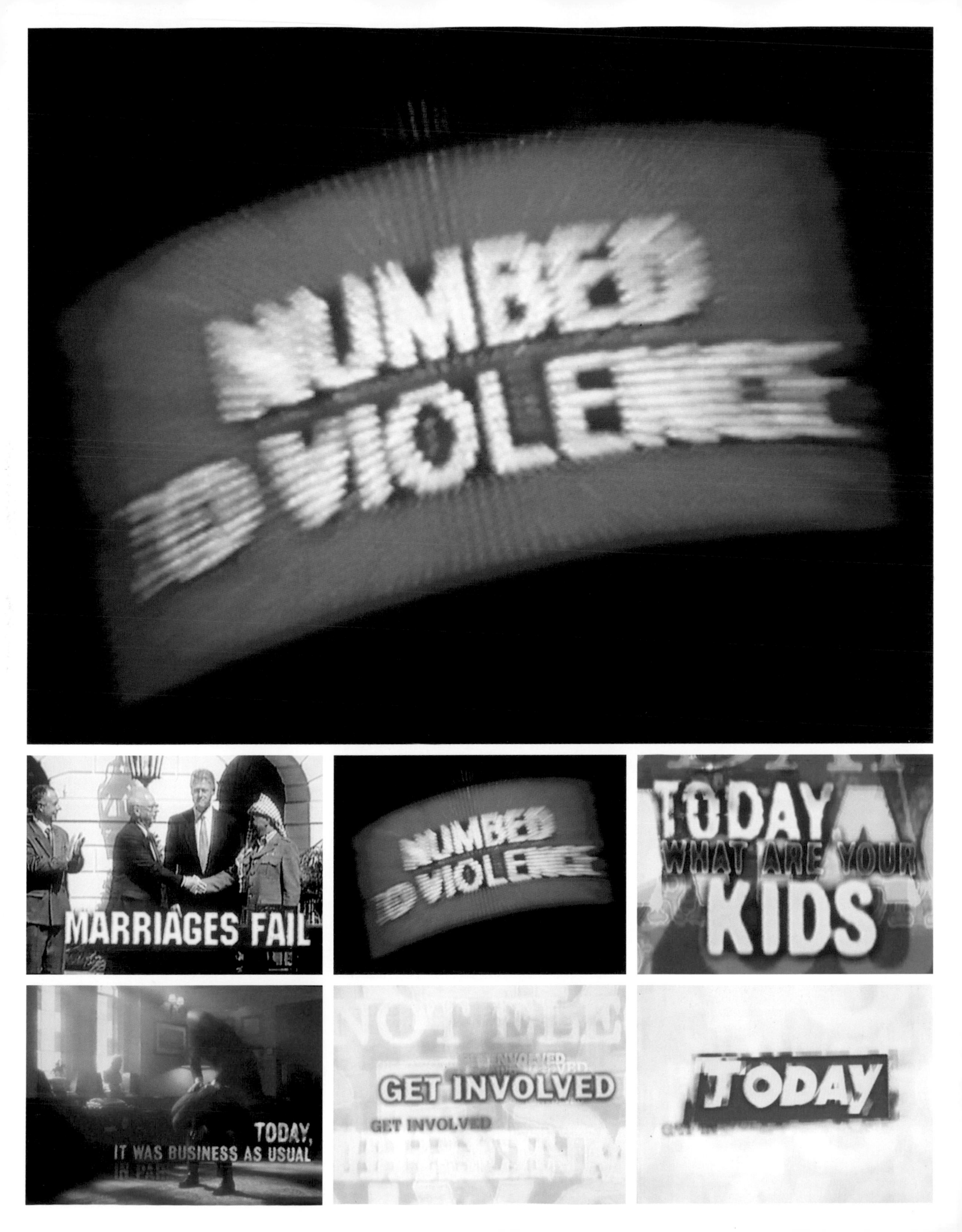

CLIENT
MIDLAND BANK

PROJECT TITLE
FIRST DIRECT

ADVERTISING AGENCY
HOWELL HENRY CHALDECOTT LURY

IDENTITY DESIGN
PAUL JARVIS
SEAN PERKINS

PROJECT DESCRIPTION
THE DESIGN OF AN IDENTITY, BANK CARDS AND LAUNCH CAMPAIGN FOR FIRST DIRECT, MIDLAND BANK'S TELEPHONE BANK, THE BANK WITHOUT BRANCHES

FIRST DIRECT

CLIENT
LLOYDS OF LONDON

PROJECT TITLE
NIGHT IDENTITY

DESIGN COMPANY
IMAGINATION

PROJECT DESCRIPTION
A SPECTACULAR LONDON LANDMARK. THIS LIGHTING DESIGN SCHEME
WAS ONE OF A NUMBER OF CREATIVE SOLUTIONS DEVISED BY
IMAGINATION TO CELEBRATE THE 300TH ANNIVERSARY OF LLOYDS OF
LONDON

LLOYDS OF LONDON

CLIENT	TITLE	DESIGN COMPANY	PROJECT DESCRIPTION
ASAHI BREWERIES	LE FLAMME D'OR	PHILIPPE STARCK	BRASSERIE, RESTAURANT, BAR AND MULTI-PURPOSE MEETING ROOMS,
	ASAHI BUILDING		TOKYO

P 88 AND 89

IN TERMS OF A CORPORATE IDENTITY IT IS
A SYMBOL OF CORPORATE HEALTH AND A
PROMISE OF THE TWENTY-FIRST CENTURY.

A VISUAL MANIFESTATION OF A BRAND,
ASAHI.

ITS SYMBOLISM EXERTS MAGNETIC
PULLING POWER UPON LARGE NUMBERS
OF VISITORS WHO COME TO EXPERIENCE
THE POWERFUL LOOKING BUILDING AND
DRINK ASAHI BEER.

CLIENT
TAUNTON CIDER

PHOTOGRAPHY
MARK ALESKY

P 90 AND 91

PROJECT TITLE
DRUM LIVE ADVERTISING 1994

ADVERTISING AGENCY
COWAN KEMSLEY TAYLOR

CREATIVES
GRAHAM CAPPI
ALAN MOSELEY

PROJECT DESCRIPTION
THE BRAND IDENTITY FOR DRUM CIDER IS BASED AROUND THE CREATION
AND EXPLOITATION OF A MUTANT DWARF CHARACTER. AN UNCONVEN-
TIONAL AND DISTURBING IMAGE WHICH HAS BEEN PROJECTED ONTO
THE BACK OF MOVING VEHICLES, MADE IMPROMPTU LIVE APPEARANCES
AND BECOME THE 'ANTI-HERO' OF PRESS/POSTER WORK

YOU'LL LOVE IT *so much*

CLIENT
BRITISH AIRWAYS

PROJECT TITLE
SURPRISE SURPRISE

ADVERTISING AGENCY
SAATCHI & SAATCHI

CREATIVES
MATT RYAN
JOHN PALLANT
MARK HANRAHAN

PRODUCTION COMPANY
PAUL WEILAND FILM CO LTD

DIRECTOR
FRANK BUDGEN

PROJECT DESCRIPTION
AT SELECTED CINEMAS BRITISH AIRWAYS RAN AUDIENCE PARTICIPATION ADS FOR THEIR
CITY BREAK COMMERCIALS. A MEMBER OF THE AUDIENCE (PLANTED BY THE ADVERTISING
AGENCY) STANDS UP IN THE MIDDLE OF THE COMMERCIAL AND INTERACTS WITH THE
CELLULOID COUPLE ON SCREEN

LEVI'S SATELLITE PARTY

CLIENT	PROJECT TITLE	CREATIVE DIRECTOR	DESIGNER	PROJECT DESCRIPTION
LEVI STRAUSS EUROPE	LEVI'S LIVE TV	SALLI HOLLINSON	PERRY WESTWOOD	LEVI'S 1993 PAN-EUROPEAN SEASON AND CAMPAIGN LAUNCH
DESIGN COMPANY	EXECUTIVE PRODUCER			
VISAGE BUSINESS TELEVISION	BOB CLARKE			

LEVI'S STAGED A SERIES OF LIVE, SATELLITE LINKED PARTIES TO LAUNCH THEIR NEW SEASON AND COMMERCIALS TO ALL STAFF AND FRANCHISES AROUND EUROPE.

'EVERYONE FROM JEANS MANUFAC-TURERS TO DESIGNER-LAGER BREWERS HAS A STYLE-LEADER ADVERTISING AND MEDIA STRATEGY, BUT, IF YOU WANT TO KEEP UP WITH THE PEOPLE WHOM OTHER PEOPLE WANT TO KEEP UP WITH, IT TAKES SOMETHING SPECIAL – AND THIS WAS IT.'

SIMON WALDMAN, MEDIA WEEK

ZOO TV

BONO HAS DEVELOPED A HABIT OF MAKING CALLS DURING THE SHOW FROM THE LIVE PHONE LINES ON STAGE.

HIGHLIGHTS INCLUDE ORDERING PIZZA FOR THE ENTIRE AUDIENCE, CALLING THE HOME SHOPPING CLUB AND LIVE SEX LINES. HE'S EVEN PLACED CALLS TO THE WHITE HOUSE AND TO JOHN MAJOR TO PROTEST ABOUT THE SELAFIELD NUCLEAR FUEL REPROCESSING PLANT.

THE EBB AND FLOW OF SUCH A VAST COLLAGE OF INFORMATION AND IMAGES FROM SO MANY DIFFERENT SOURCES CREATES THE EFFECT OF CHANNEL-ZAPPING ON AN URBAN SCALE.

LIVE

CLIENT	PROJECT TITLE	DESIGN COMPANY	LIGHTING DIRECTOR	VIDEO DIRECTOR
U2	ZOO TV OUTSIDE BROADCAST	FISHER PARK	PETER WILLIAMS	CAROL DODDS
	1992 WORLD TOUR			
		DESIGNERS		
		MARK FISHER		
		JONATHAN PARK		

P 100 AND 101 (98 AND 99 PREVIOUS)

CLIENT
MTV EUROPE

TITLES
SAVE FUEL
FUEL

FAST FOOD
HAIR

DESIGN COMPANY
FUEL

PROJECT DESCRIPTION
THREE THIRTY-SECOND IMAGE SPOTS 1994

DESIGNERS
PETER MILES
DAMON MURRAY
STEPHEN SORRELL

P 102 AND 103

'NOWADAYS PEOPLES' VISUAL IMAGINA-
TION IS SO MUCH MORE SOPHISTICATED,
SO MUCH MORE DEVELOPED, PARTICU-
LARLY IN YOUNG PEOPLE, THAT NOW
YOU CAN MAKE AN IMAGE WHICH JUST
SLIGHTLY SUGGESTS SOMETHING, THEY
CAN MAKE OF IT WHAT THEY WILL.'

ROBERT DOISNEAU

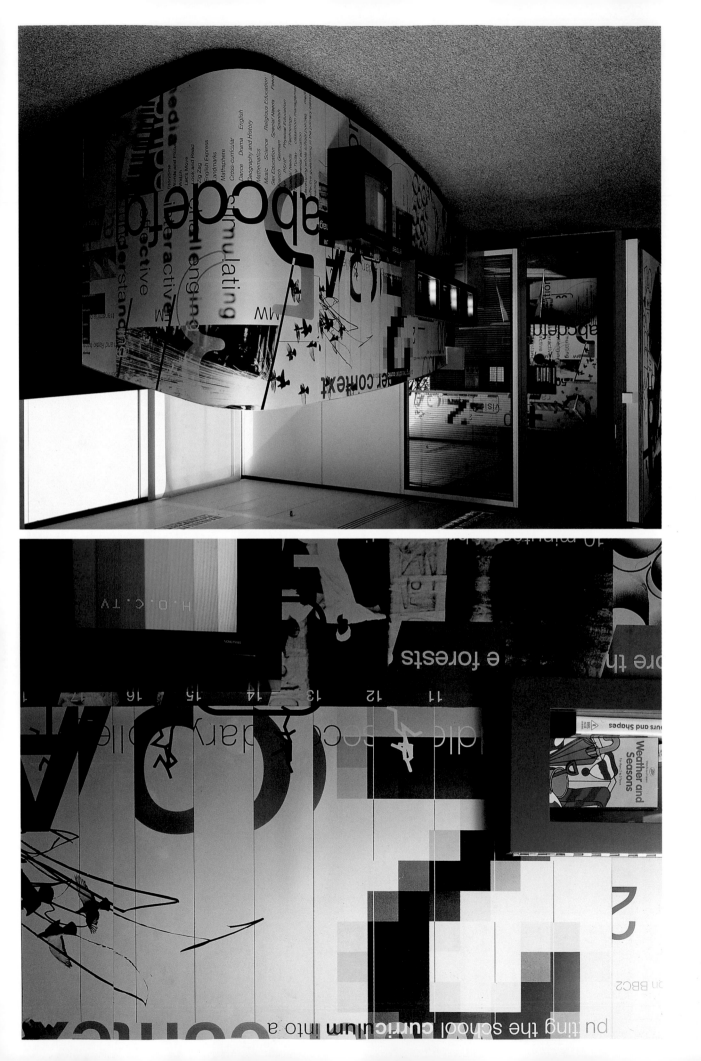

'THE DESIGN PROVIDES BBC SCHOOL TELE-VISION WITH A HIGHLY ANIMATED VISUAL IDENTITY THAT BEFITS AN ORGANISATION WORKING AT THE FOREFRONT OF MEDIA TECHNOLOGY. THE EXUBERANCE OF VISUAL ACTIVITY IS APPROPRIATE FOR A COMPANY DISTRIBUTING VISUAL AND ACOUSTIC MATERIAL THAT EDUCATES AND INSPIRES MORE YOUNG PEOPLE ALL OVER THE WORLD THAN ANY OTHER BROADCASTING COMPANY.'

NICK BELL

CLIENT	DESIGN COMPANY	INTERIOR DESIGNERS	PROJECT DESCRIPTION
BBC SCHOOL TELEVISION	NICK BELL	CASSON MANN	TYPOGRAPHIC SKIN TO COVER THE WALLS OF AN OFFICE AT BBC SCHOOL TELEVISION, WHITE CITY, LONDON 1993

P 104 AND 105

CLIENT	PROJECT TITLE	DESIGN COMPANY	PROJECT DESCRIPTION
SABA	JIM NATURE	THOMSON – DESIGN CENTRE	WOODEN TV 1993

THE TELEVISION SHELL IS MADE OF WOOD AND CAN BE RECYCLED

DESIGNER
PHILIPPE STARCK

ONE OF THE FIRST PRODUCTS DESIGNED BY PHILIPPE STARCK FOR THE FRENCH ELECTRICAL COMPANY THOMSON GROUP.

THE PET SHOP BOYS VIDEO, 'LIBERATION,' CAN BE EXPERIENCED THROUGH THE WORLD OF VIRTUAL REALITY AND ARTI-FICIAL NATURE.

CLIENT	PROJECT TITLE	DESIGN COMPANY	3D ANIMATION	PROJECT DESCRIPTION
WHY NOT FILMS PET SHOP BOYS	LIBERATION 1994	FUTURE REALITY LTD	IAN BIRD	3D COMPUTER ANIMATION AND MOTION SIMULATOR 1994

SIMULATION
IAN WILLIAMS

CLIENT	PROJECT TITLE	DESIGN COMPANIES	PRODUCT DESIGNER	PROJECT DESCRIPTION
PET SHOP BOYS	VERY PET SHOP BOYS	PENTAGRAM	DANIEL WEIL	CD PACKAGE 1993
PARTNERSHIP		FARROW		
			PHOTOGRAPHY	
	GRAPHIC DESIGNERS	CHRIS NASH	
	MARK FARROW		
	ROB PETRIE		

PET SHOP BOYS

CLIENT
IBM DIRECT

PROJECT TITLE
48 SHEET BILLBOARD 1994

DESIGN AND PHOTOGRAPHY
MALCOLM GOLDIE

PROJECT DESCRIPTION
TO HELP PROJECT IBM'S BELIEF IN THE FUSION OF INDUSTRY AND ART, THE COMPANY ISSUED A BRIEF TO LONDON'S ROYAL COLLEGE OF ART TO DESIGN A 48 SHEET BILLBOARD WHICH INCORPORATED THE IBM DIRECT TELEPHONE NUMBER. SEVEN DESIGNS WERE CHOSEN AND PLACED AT PROMINENT SITES AROUND ENGLAND FOR A PERIOD OF TWO MONTHS. THIS DESIGN INTERPRETS THE TELEPHONE NUMBER IN THE FORM OF A MODULAR GRID WHERE EACH RECTANGLE IS EITHER POSITIVE OR NEGATIVE TO REFLECT THE BINARY NUMBER SYSTEM. THE DOG STANDS IN THE LUGGAGE COMPARTMENT OF A NUMBER 31 BUS. ITS BREED AND OWNER ARE UNKNOWN

CLIENT
METROPOLITAN POLICE

PROJECT TITLE
HIGASHI-NIHONBASHI
POLICE BOX

ARCHITECT
ATSUSHI KITAGAWARA & ILCD

PROJECT DESCRIPTION
POLICE BOX 1992

PHOTOGRAPHY
SHIGEO OGAWA SHINKENCHIKU©

POLICE BOX

DESIGN COMPANY
STUDIO DUMBAR

PHOTOGRAPHY
LEX VAN PIETERSON

CAPTIONS
1
2
3

CLIENT
KONINKLIJKE MARECHAUSSEE 1, 2
DUTCH POLICE 3

PROJECT DESCRIPTION
DAY AND NIGHT REFLECTION
1993
CORPORATE IDENTITY
1993

P 118 AND 119

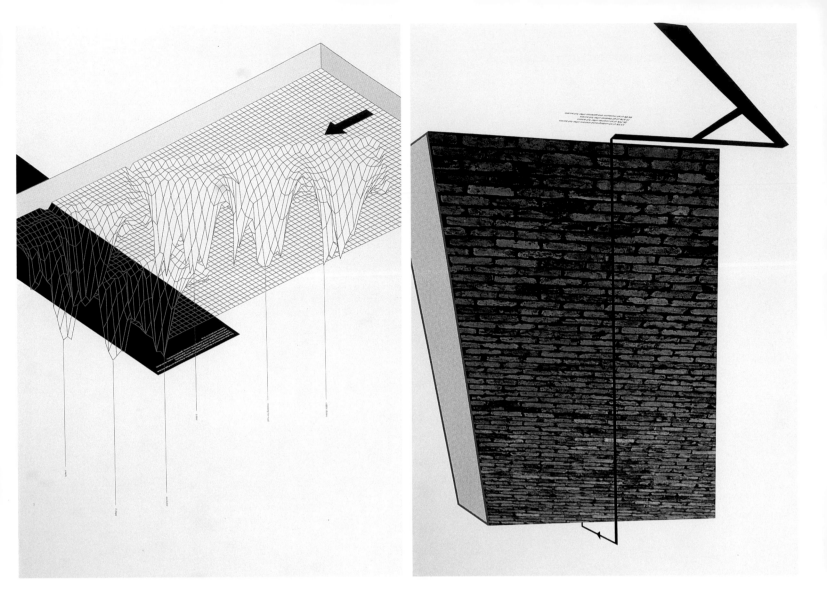

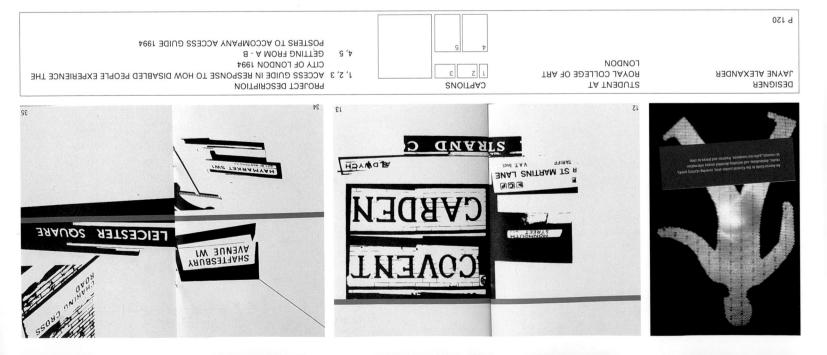

DESIGNER
JAYNE ALEXANDER

STUDENT AT
ROYAL COLLEGE OF ART
LONDON

CAPTIONS

PROJECT DESCRIPTION
1, 2, 3   ACCESS GUIDE IN RESPONSE TO HOW DISABLED PEOPLE EXPERIENCE THE
CITY OF LONDON 1994
4, 5   GETTING FROM A - B
POSTERS TO ACCOMPANY ACCESS GUIDE 1994

IN AUTUMN 1992 SDU TAPPAN WAS COMMISSIONED TO DESIGN MARKINGS FOR THE GLASS WINDOWS OF THE DUTCH PARLIAMENT BUILDING ESPECIALLY FOR VISUALLY HANDICAPPED PERSONS.

THE DESIGN DISTINGUISHES ITSELF FROM OTHER STANDARD SOLUTIONS BECAUSE IT GIVES THE TEXT OF ARTICLE 1 OF THE DUTCH CONSTITUTION IN BRAILLE. ARTICLE 1 OF THE DUTCH CONSTITUTION DECLARES EACH PERSON IN THE NETHERLANDS EQUAL BEFORE THE LAW.

CLIENT
THE MINISTRY OF HOUSING
AND CONSTRUCTION

DESIGN COMPANY
SDU TAPPAN

PRODUCTION
BRUNS BV

DESIGNERS
JORGE STEENBERGEN
ALBERT HENNIPMAN

PHOTOGRAPHY
LIGHTHART & VAN AARSEN

PROJECT DESCRIPTION
BRAILLE SAFETY RIBBON FOR THE NEW DUTCH PARLIAMENT BUILDING 1993

P 122 AND 123

CLIENT	PROJECT TITLE	DESIGN COMPANY	PHOTOGRAPHY	PROJECT DESCRIPTION
DUTCH PARLIAMENT	PORTRAIT GALLERY	SDU TAPPAN	DIETER SCHUTTE	INTERACTIVE INFORMATION DESK
	PRODUCTION	DESIGNERS		
	BRUNS BV	JORGE STEENBERGEN		
		ALBERT HENNIPMAN		

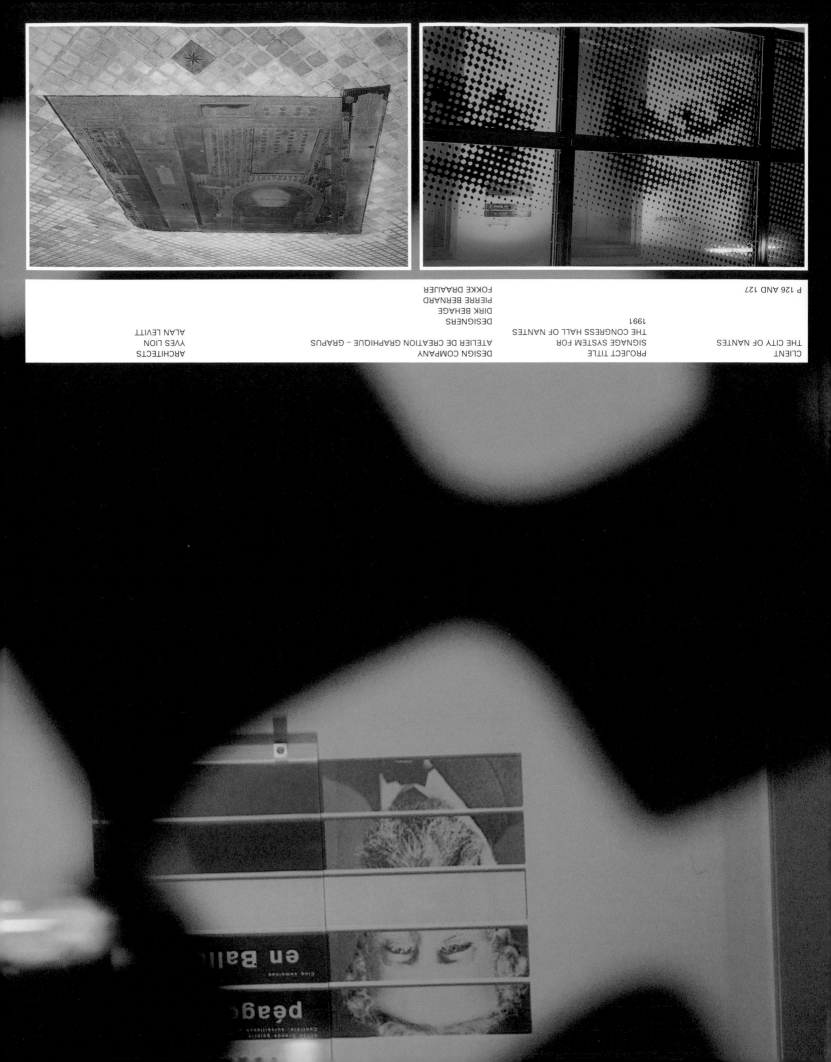

CLIENT
THE CITY OF NANTES

PROJECT TITLE
SIGNAGE SYSTEM FOR
THE CONGRESS HALL OF NANTES
1991

DESIGN COMPANY
ATELIER DE CRÉATION GRAPHIQUE – GRAPUS

DESIGNERS
DIRK BEHAGE
PIERRE BERNARD
FOKKE DRAAIJER

ARCHITECTS
YVES LION
ALAN LEVITT

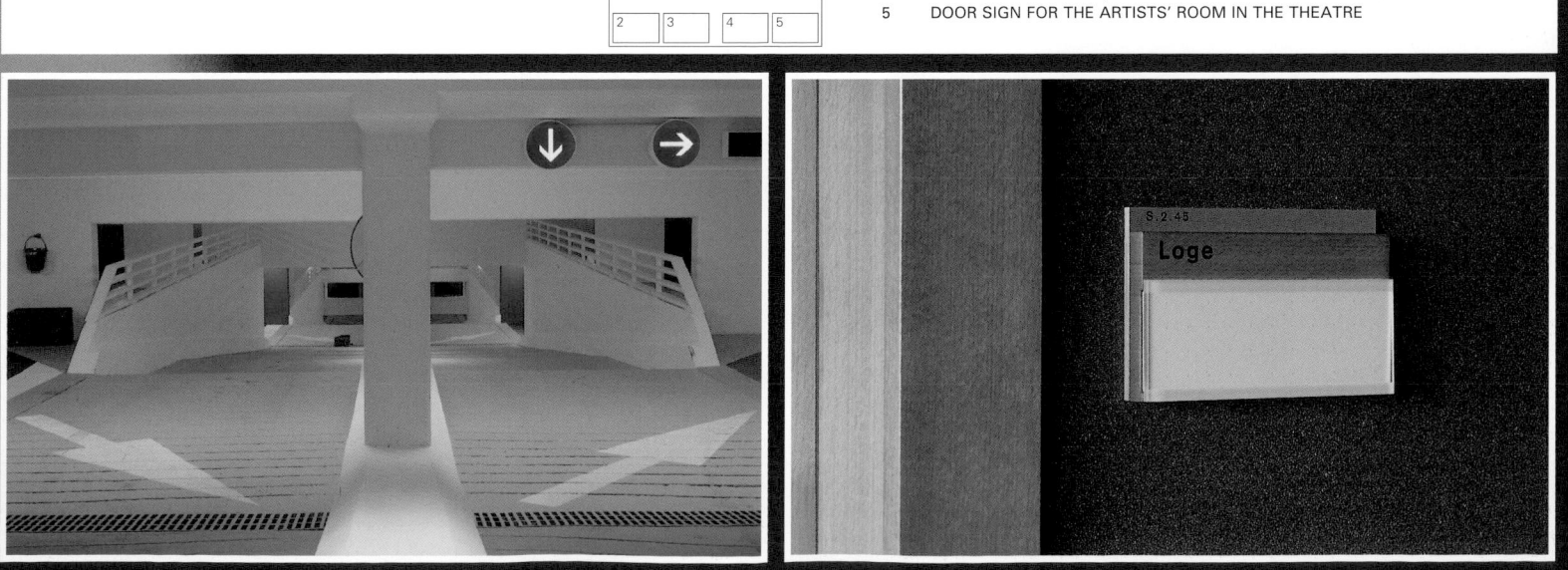

CAPTIONS

1   SIGN SHOWING COLOURS AND IMAGES FOR EACH FLOOR OF THE CAR PARK
2   DETAIL OF A PORTRAIT OF JULES VERNE (A WRITER BORN IN NANTES)
3   4 X 4M CAST-IRON PLATE PLAN OF THE BUILDING AND GARDEN
4   CAR PARK ENTRANCE, HERE YOU CAN SEE THE COLOURS OF EACH LEVEL
5   DOOR SIGN FOR THE ARTISTS' ROOM IN THE THEATRE

Conception Müller & Création Graphique '76 · Cegna · Imprimerie Ambérieul

CLIENT
THE NATIONAL PARKS
OF FFANCE

PROJECT TITLE
GRAPHIC IDENTITY FOR
THE NATIONAL PARKS OF FRANCE
1990 TO PRESENT

DESIGN COMPANY
ATELIER DE CREATION GRAPHIQUE – GRAPUS

DESIGNERS
DIRK BEHAGE
PIERRE BERNARD
FOKKE DRAAIJER

PROJECT DESCRIPTION
A GRAPHICAL REPRESENTATION OF THE NATIONAL PARKS AND EVERYTHING IN THEM
BECOMES THE INSPIRATION FOR THE VISUAL IDENTITY OF THE PARKS

CAPTIONS

1	2
	3
	4

1   EMBLEM REPRESENTING 7 PARKS
2   INTERNAL POSTER TO PRESENT THE EMBLEM OF THE 7 PARKS
3   POSTER CELEBRATING THE 30TH ANNIVERSARY OF THE NATIONAL PARKS
4   INTERNAL POSTER TO PRESENT THE GRAPHIC IDENTITY AND THE SIGNAGE SYSTEM

P 128 AND 129

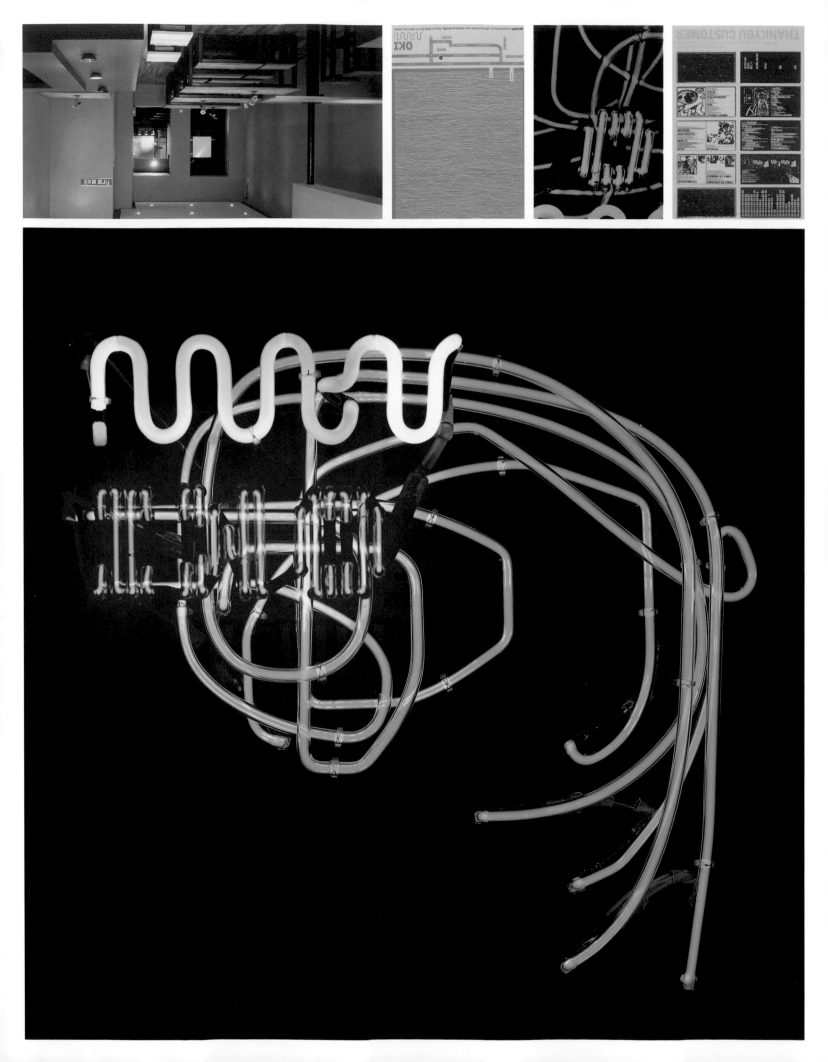

LUNCHTIME 12.00–14.30

EVENING 18.00–23.30

10,000 VOLTS
DANGER DO NOT TOUCH

CLIENT
OKI-NAMI

PROJECT TITLE
OKI-NAMI (BIG WAVE)

DESIGN COMPANY
GRAPHIC THOUGHT FACILITY

DESIGNERS
PAUL NEALE
ANDREW STEVENS

PHOTOGRAPHY
ANDREW PENKETH

PROJECT DESCRIPTION
RESTAURANT IDENTITY

CLIENT
ALAN YAU-WAGAMAMA LTD

PROJECT TITLE
WAGAMAMA

ARCHITECT
JSP ARCHITECTS
MICHAEL STIFF
RICHARD BLANDY
AND JOHN PAWSON

PHOTOGRAPHY
MATTHEW WEINREB

PROJECT DESCRIPTION
NOODLE BAR, BLOOMSBURY
LONDON 1992

POSITIVE EATING
POSITIVE LIVING

'MUJI SELLS PRODUCTS THAT ARE WELL MADE AND MADE OF QUALITY MATERIALS.

WE TRY TO OFFER THESE PRODUCTS AT REASONABLE COST.

WE AVOID FUSSY OR UNNECESSARY OVER DESIGN.

WE PRESENT OUR PRODUCTS SIMPLY IN SHOPS WITH BASIC SHELVING.
THE PRODUCTS SHOULD BE EASY TO SEE.

THERE IS NO MUJI LOGO ON ANY PRODUCT.

THERE ARE OVER 200 MUJI OUTLETS IN JAPAN, 5 IN HONG KONG, 4 IN THE UK.'

CLIENT
MUJIRUSHI RYOHIN EUROPE

PROJECT TITLE
NO BRAND GOODS

ARCHITECT (UK)
HARPER MCKAY LTD

P 134 AND 135

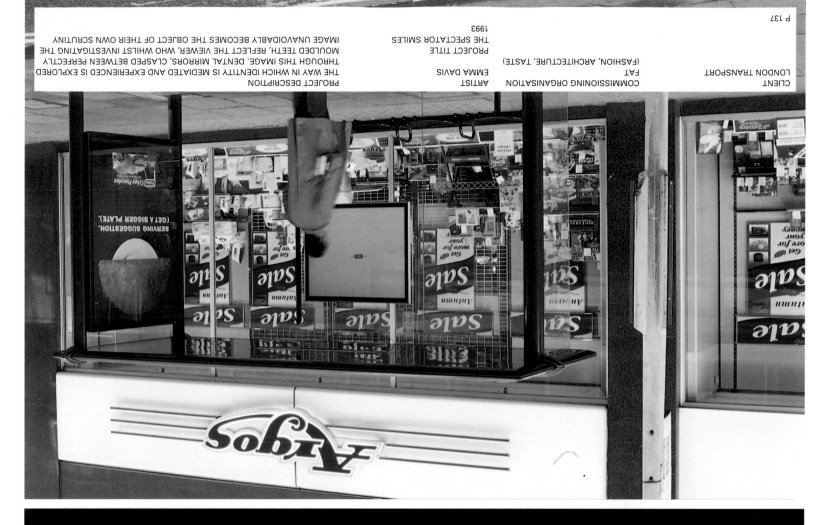

CLIENT
LONDON TRANSPORT

COMMISSIONING ORGANISATION
FAT
(FASHION, ARCHITECTURE, TASTE)

ARTIST
EMMA DAVIS

PROJECT TITLE
THE SPECTATOR SMILES
1993

PROJECT DESCRIPTION
THE WAY IN WHICH IDENTITY IS MEDIATED AND EXPERIENCED IS EXPLORED THROUGH THIS IMAGE. DENTAL MIRRORS, CLASPED BETWEEN PERFECTLY MOULDED TEETH, REFLECT THE VIEWER, WHO WHILST INVESTIGATING THE IMAGE UNAVOIDABLY BECOMES THE OBJECT OF THEIR OWN SCRUTINY

ARTSITE IS A PROJECT THAT UTILISES THE BUS SHELTER TO PROMOTE COLLABORATION BETWEEN PRACTITIONERS OF DIFFERENT VISUAL DISCIPLINES WITH AN EMPHASIS TOWARDS NEW CONCEPTUAL AND CRITICAL TENDENCIES IN THE VISUAL ARTS. THE BENEFITS OF THIS COLLABORATION WILL BE TO CHALLENGE EXISTING NOTIONS OF WHAT IS PERCEIVED TO BE PUBLIC ART.

CLIENT
BUS STOP

COMMISSIONING ORGANISATION
FAT

ARTIST
CLIVE SALL

PROJECT TITLE
PERFORMANCE SPECIFICATION
1993

PROJECT DESCRIPTION
THE REPRESENTATION OF A YOUNG GIRL IS JUXTAPOSED WITH AN EYE
TEST THAT WAS USED TO DETERMINE ARYAN QUALITIES IN NAZI OCCU-
PIED POLAND. ALTHOUGH THE GIRL SEEMS TO FIT THE PRESCRIPTION,
THE 'PERFECT' MATCH IS ALWAYS UNOBTAINABLE AS SHE IS RENDERED IN
COLOUR AND THE EYE TEST IS RENDERED IN BLACK AND WHITE

ARTIST
DINA BURNSTOCK

PROJECT TITLE
UNTITLED
1993

PROJECT DESCRIPTION
TWO FEET CRUSHED WITHIN A JAR SYMBOLISE PERSONAL OBSESSION
WITH PHYSICAL PRESERVATION. THE IMAGE EXPLORES A SHIFT IN SOCIETY,
AWAY FROM THE SEARCH FOR ONE'S 'TRUE' SELF TOWARDS THE DESIRE
TO CREATE AN IDEALISED AND RECONSTRUCTED SELF

PROJECT TITLE
HAND TO MOUTH
1993

ARTIST
RACHAEL ATHERTON

PROJECT DESCRIPTION
THIS IMAGE EXPLORES EXTREMITIES OF FEMALE EXPERIENCE. THE VIEWER IS 'OFFERED' A TASTE OF FEMININITY REPRESENTED AS A SPOONFUL OF DELICIOUS STICKY-SWEET SEXUAL PLEASURE AND FOUL DOMESTIC DRUDGERY

CLIENT
LONDON TRANSPORT

COMMISSIONING ORGANISATION
FAT

ARTIST
CAROLINE KING

PROJECT TITLE
UNTITLED
1993

PROJECT DESCRIPTION
AN AT ONCE FAMILIAR YET UNRECOGNISABLE IMAGE UTILISES THE MEDIA AND LANGUAGE OF ADVERTISING TO PRESENT THE VIEWER WITH AN ABSTRACT AND SUMPTUOUS PRODUCT CREATED TO SATISFY CONSUMER DEMAND

THE PHYSICAL IMPOSSIBILITY OF DEATH IN THE MIND OF SOMEONE LIVING

ARTIST	TITLE	PROJECT DESCRIPTION
DAMIEN HIRST	THE PHYSICAL IMPOSSIBILITY OF DEATH IN THE MIND OF SOMEONE LIVING 1991	GLASS, STEEL, SILICONE, SHARK, FORMALDEHYDE SOLUTION

P 140 AND 141 (PREVIOUS)

ARTIST	TITLE	PROJECT DESCRIPTION
DAMIEN HIRST	SOME WENT MAD, SOME RAN AWAY FROM THE FLOCK 1994	GLASS, STEEL, SILICONE, LAMB, FORMALDEHYDE SOLUTION

P 142

ARTIST
DAMIEN HIRST

TITLE
MOTHER AND CHILD DIVIDED
1993

PROJECT DESCRIPTION
GLASS, STEEL, GRP COMPOSITES, SILICONE, COW, CALF, FORMALDEHYDE
SOLUTION

CLIENTS
LWT PROGRAMMES LTD
NORDOFF-ROBBINS
NINTENDO

P 144 AND 145

PROJECT DESCRIPTION
AS THE COCA-COLA COMPANY FACES INTENSE GLOBAL COMPETITION FROM RETAILER OWN-LABEL COLAS, THE REST OF THE CARBONATED SOFT DRINKS MARKET MUST CONSIDER THE GROWING POTENTIAL FOR A TV GAMESHOW, ROCK GROUP OR COMPUTER GAMES CHARACTER TO PROVIDE A SERIOUS COMPETITIVE THREAT

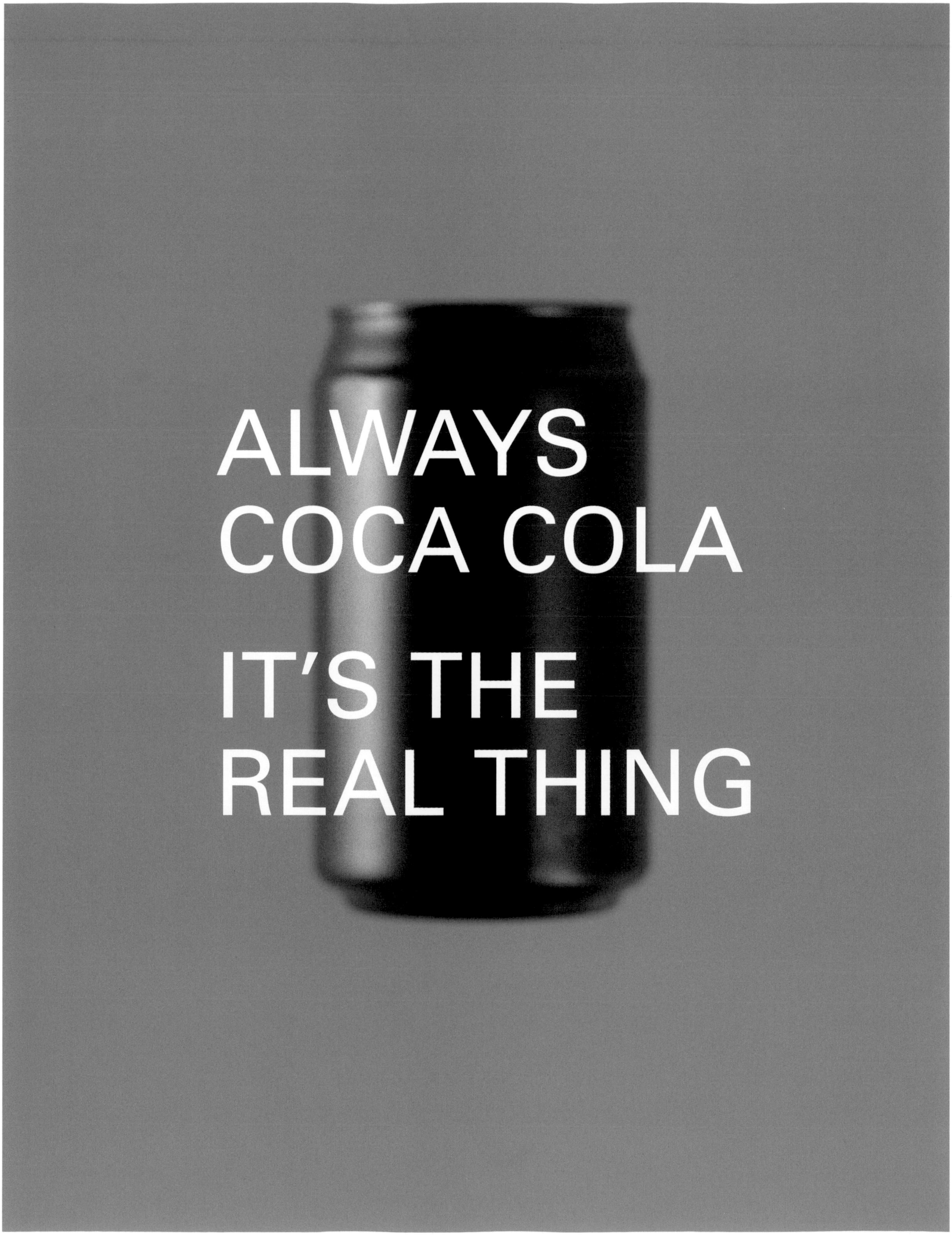
ALWAYS
COCA COLA
IT'S THE
REAL THING

CLIENT
THE COCA-COLA COMPANY

PROJECT TITLE
THE WORLD OF COCA-COLA
ATLANTA, USA

PHOTOGRAPHY
TIMOTHY HURSLEY

PROJECT DESCRIPTION
IN THE BRAND'S HOMETOWN OF ATLANTA THE WORLD OF COCA-COLA
PROVIDES A 'SHRINE' TO THE HERITAGE, VALUES AND ASPIRATIONS OF
THE WORLD'S BEST-KNOWN BRAND

P 146 AND 147

COMPANY
SEGA ENTERPRISES LTD

PROJECT TITLE
JOYPOLIS

LOCATION
YOKOHAMA, JAPAN

P 148 AND 149

PROJECT DESCRIPTION
OPENED ON JULY 20 1994, JOYPOLIS REPRESENTS THE BIRTH OF A NEW
GENERATION OF LEISURE FACILITIES BASED ON THE CONCEPT OF 'INTERACTIVE
ENTERTAINMENT' AND MAKING FULL USE OF SEGA'S NEWEST AND MOST
ADVANCED TECHNOLOGY

CAPTIONS

1   SOFTWARE FOR VR-1
2   VR-1
3   GHOST HUNTERS
4   INSIDE JOYPOLIS
5   RAIL CHASE RIDE

CLIENT
EURODISNEY

PROJECT TITLE
TOURING SLEEPING BEAUTY
CASTLE

DESIGN COMPANY
IMAGINATION

PROJECT DESCRIPTION
BRINGING THE MAGIC OF EURODISNEY TO SIXTEEN EUROPEAN CITIES IN
SIXTEEN WEEKS, THIS SCALE REPLICA OF THE SLEEPING BEAUTY CASTLE
WAS DESIGNED TO HIGHLY EXACTING LOCAL STANDARDS, NIGHTLY FIREWORK
DISPLAYS MADE A DRAMATIC LOCAL PRESENTATION, WHILE WITHIN THE CASTLE
THE CREATIVE AUDIO-VISUAL PRESENTATION INTRODUCED THE NEW
RESORT TO ITS TARGET AUDIENCE

A COLLECTION OF WEED PLANTS WERE PRESERVED IN VINEGAR AFTER BEING GATHERED FROM THE BORDERS OF EURODISNEY. THE BOTTLES ARE MAPPED OUT ACCORDING TO THE LAYOUT OF EURODISNEY WITH EACH OF THE ATTRAC-TION NAMES SANDBLASTED ONTO THE BOTTLES. SEEDS WERE ALSO COLLECTED FROM THE 48 DIFFERENT WEEDS AND PLANTED AT EACH OF THE CORRESPOND-ING SITES INSIDE EURODISNEY.

ARTISTS
KATE ERICSON
MEL ZIEGLER

PROJECT TITLE
VINEGAR OF THE 48 WEEDS
1992

CAPTIONS

1, 2   WEEDS, VINEGAR, SANDBLASTED GLASS, STEEL SHELVES, 211 X 234 X 13CM
        PHOTOGRAPHY JOHN RIDDY, LONDON
        COURTESY LISSON GALLERY, LONDON
3   THE ARTISTS PLANTING SEEDS AT EURODISNEY 1992
        COURTESY MICHAEL KLEIN GALLERY, NEW YORK

P 152 AND 153

A MAGAZINE CREATED, WRITTEN,
DESIGNED AND PHOTOGRAPHICALLY
DOCUMENTED USING AGFA DIGITAL
COMPUTER EQUIPMENT IN THE BACK OF
A VOLKSWAGEN VAN, WHILE DRIVING
ACROSS EUROPE.

'WE'RE TRAVELLING ACROSS EUROPE IN
A VOLKSWAGEN VAN MAKING A MAGA-
ZINE CALLED TWENTY-SIX.

THE MAGAZINE IS NOT ONLY ABOUT
TYPOGRAPHY, COMMUNICATION AND
TECHNOLOGY, IT'S A MAGAZINE ABOUT
PROCESS: THE PROCESS OF MAKING A
MAGAZINE.

WE WILL FIND OUT WHAT THIS MAGAZINE
IS ABOUT AS WE GO ALONG.
FINDING OUT IS PART OF THE PROCESS.'

CLIENT	PROJECT TITLE	CREATIVE DIRECTOR	DESIGN STUDIO	COMPUTER IMAGING/TYPOGRAPHY
AGFA COMPUGRAPHIC	26, VOL 1, NO 2	ROBERT MANLEY	KOEPKE DESIGN GROUP	MICHAEL TARDIF
PUBLISHER	ADVERTISING AGENCY	MANAGING EDITOR	DESIGN & ART DIRECTION	ASSISTANT PHOTOGRAPHER
PETER MILLER	ALTMAN & MANLEY	ELIZABETH HENDERSON MILDE	GARY KEHDE	NIELS COOGAN LEPPERT
	EAGLE ADVERTISING			

P 154 AND 155 (156 AND 157 OVERLEAF)

I'm with Margaret Thatcher on this one. I don't think Europe should have a single currency. It would eliminate one of travel's most satisfying routines, the changing of money. It's like a cleansing ritual. You purge your system of England and all things English by converting your pounds into guilders. You shed Holland by exchanging your guilders for francs. And francs for Deutch marks and Deutch marks for Swiss francs and Swiss francs for whatever it is they use in Czechoslovakia. It's how you know you've left one place and arrived in another. Especially since crossing within the European Community, crossing from Belgium to France on a major highway feels no different than crossing from Massachusetts to New York on the Mass Pike.

Right now, it's Friday morning and we are in Paris. We arrived last night after a swift drive through Belgium and the north of France. Somehow, it seems reasonable to drive a hundred miles an hour when the speedometer is in kilometers. Somehow the speed doesn't feel real because we're moving in metric units. And the spending doesn't feel real either because we're doing it in guilders or francs rather than dollars.

25

echtheidskenmerken

let op de vier

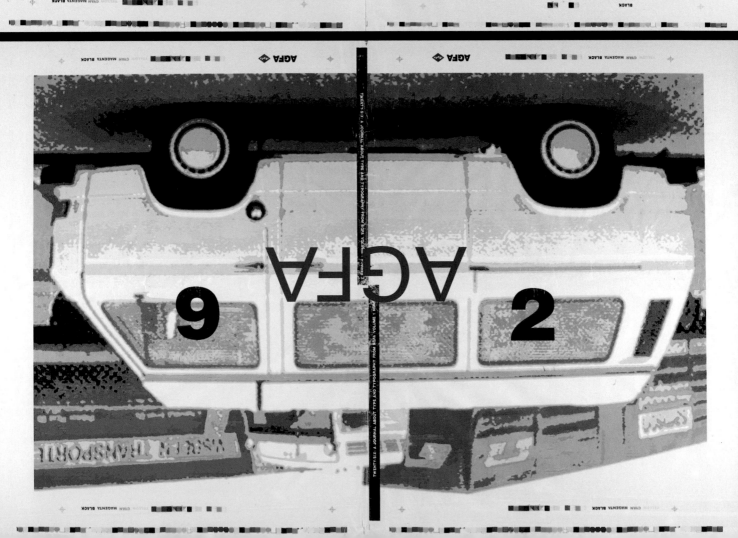

AGFA

9   2

rebellion
chaos
order
the Swiss!

THIS END UP · UP · FRONT · SIDE UP · HAUT · ALTO · UP · ERKER BERUH... · ...RNEUERUNG · NEUEINKLEIDUNG · ZUSAMMENLEGUNG · EINBAU

We're travelling across Europe in a Volkswagen van making a magazine called twenty-six.

Yesterday, our first day on the road, we sat in a restaurant outside Victoria Station called the American Pancake House. It was a bad restaurant, but it was the only place we could get breakfast after 10 on a Sunday morning. The British, apparently, do not brunch. In England, we learned, they serve their eggs one way—fried—and they serve them with beans. In England, they put bananas and butterscotch sauce on pancakes and call it Banana Glory, at least they do this at the American Pancake House.

We sat around all jet-lagged and groggy, not eating much and trying to figure out what this magazine is really about. We know that it's about typography and communication and technology, but what does that mean in real terms. Like, what are we all going to do on this trip?

We were too tired to come up with many answers. Except that this isn't a magazine about typog-raphy as much as it's a magazine about process: the process of makingamagazine. We will find out what this magazine is about as we go along. Finding out is part of the process.

MIND THE GAP. This is our first phrase in British. It means, roughly, "watch your step when you get off the underground because there is a very small amount of space between the edge of the train and the platform and we would be very sorry if you hurt yourself." MIND THE GAP. Use it three times and it's yours. Someone thought the announcement on the train said, "It's my baguette." Perhaps that's what they say in Paris, on the Metro.

We're not a hundred percent sure about what we're doing, but we will try to mind the gap.

Today is Wednesday, November 2. I'm in a hotel on the Keizersgracht, a canal in Amsterdam. I'm trying to write about things that happened in London the day before yesterday and the day before that. It's not easy because, when you're travelling, time is very different. When it is still morning in London, it is already afternoon here. Time is amorphous and gooey. Time expands and contracts in very peculiar ways. Days have no proper beginnings and endings, and an incredible amount seems to happen within these elastic days.

THE NIKE TOWN CONCEPT COMBINES SPORTS, FITNESS, HISTORY, PRODUCT INNOVATION AND ENTERTAINMENT, TO PROVIDE A UNIQUE RETAIL BRAND EXPERIENCE.

NIKE TOWN WAS BORN OF A DESIRE BY NIKE TO EXPERIMENT WITH HOW NIKE PRODUCT WAS DISPLAYED AND MERCHANDISED.

EACH NIKE TOWN HAS A CENTRAL AREA THAT FREQUENTLY SERVES AS THE LOCATION FOR INSTORE EVENTS, ATHLETE APPEARANCES AND SPORTS-RELATED SEMINARS.

THE NIKE TOWN ENVIRONMENT ALSO FEATURES LIFESIZE STATUES OF SUPER-STAR ATHLETES AND A WIDE RANGE OF SPORS-RELATED AUDIO-VISUAL PRESENTATIONS.

NIKE TOWN IS A SPORTS RETAIL THEATRE THAT SHOWCASES NIKE'S RICH SPORTS HERITAGE, WHILE ALSO SERVING AS A VALUABLE COMMUNITY RESOURCE FOR LOCAL SPORTS AND FITNESS ACTIVITIES.

ALL NIKE TOWNS SHARE A NUMBER OF KEY PHYSICAL ELEMENTS – HIGH-TECH MULTI-MEDIA PRESENTATIONS, SPORTS MEMORABILIA FROM THE WORLD'S TOP ATHLETES AND INNOVATIVE INTERIOR DESIGN AND RETAIL FIXTURES.

HOWEVER, DESPITE THEIR SIMILAR PRINCIPALS, EACH NIKE TOWN HAS AN ENTIRELY DIFFERENT ATMOSPHERE.

CLIENT	PROJECT TITLE	DESIGN COMPANY	ARCHITECTS	PHOTOGRAPHY
NIKE	NIKE TOWN	NIKE DESIGN	GORDON THOMPSON	STEVE HALL
			JOHN FARNUM	HEDRICH BLESSING
			BRITT BREWER	

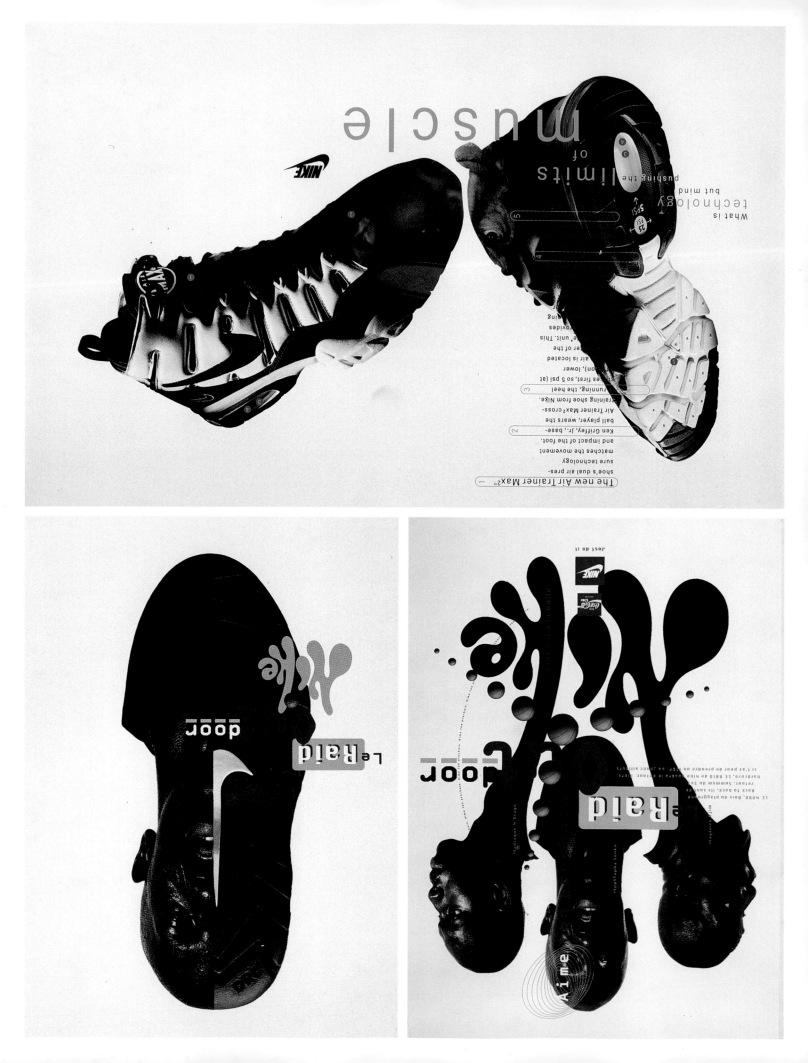

CLIENT	ADVERTISING AGENCY	CAPTIONS		PROJECT DESCRIPTION	CREATIVES
NIKE FRANCE	WIEDEN & KENNEDY		1, 2	POSTER AND BROCHURE FOR	ERNEST LUPPINACCI
				A NIKE SPONSORED FRANCE	MICHAEL PRIEVE & BOB MOORE
	DESIGNER			OUTDOOR BASKETBALL	
	ROBERT NAKATA			TOURNAMENT, 1994	PHOTOGRAPHY
					NORBERT SCHOERNER
					HANS PIETERSE

CLIENT			PROJECT DESCRIPTION	CREATIVES
NIKE USA		3	ADVERTISEMENT FOR NIKE	DAN WIEDEN & SUSAN HOFFMAN
			AIR MAX SHOES 1994	STEVE DUNN
				PHOTOGRAPHY
				HANS PIETERSE
P 162 AND 163				VARIOUS

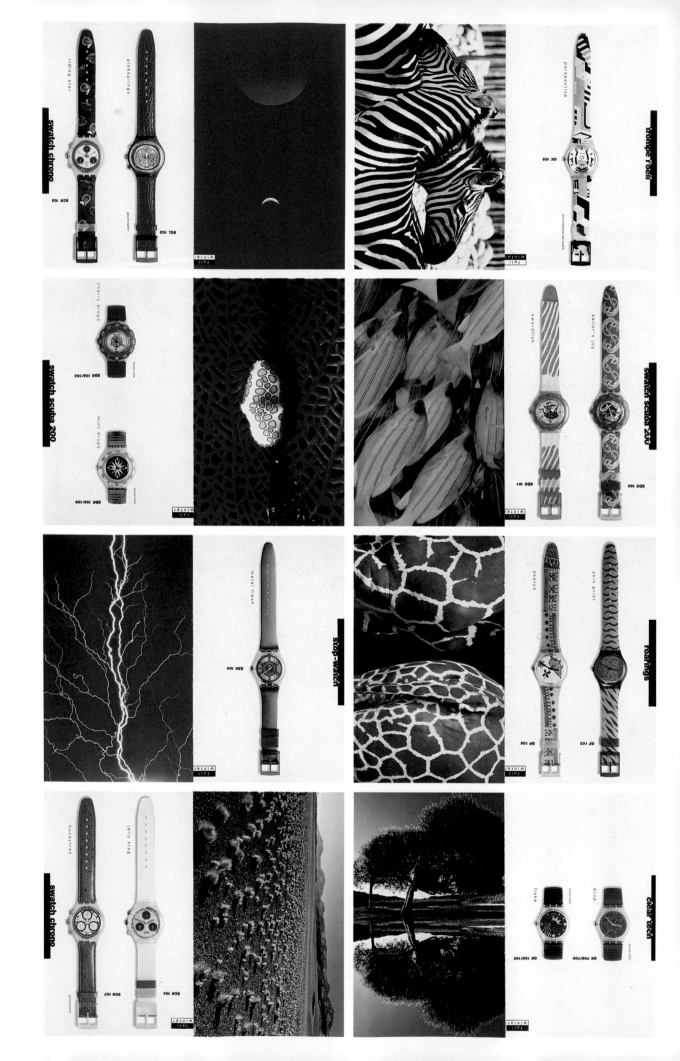

CLIENT
SWATCH

PROJECT TITLE
FALL/WINTER COLLECTION 1993 - 1994

PROJECT DESCRIPTION
SEASONAL PRODUCT LITERATURE
THE INSPIRATION BEHIND SWATCH: GREENTIC OR PINKSPRINGS, ALABAMA
OR WINDMILL, A MYRIAD OF DIFFERENT WAYS TO COLOUR A FRACTION OF
A SECOND

SWATCH

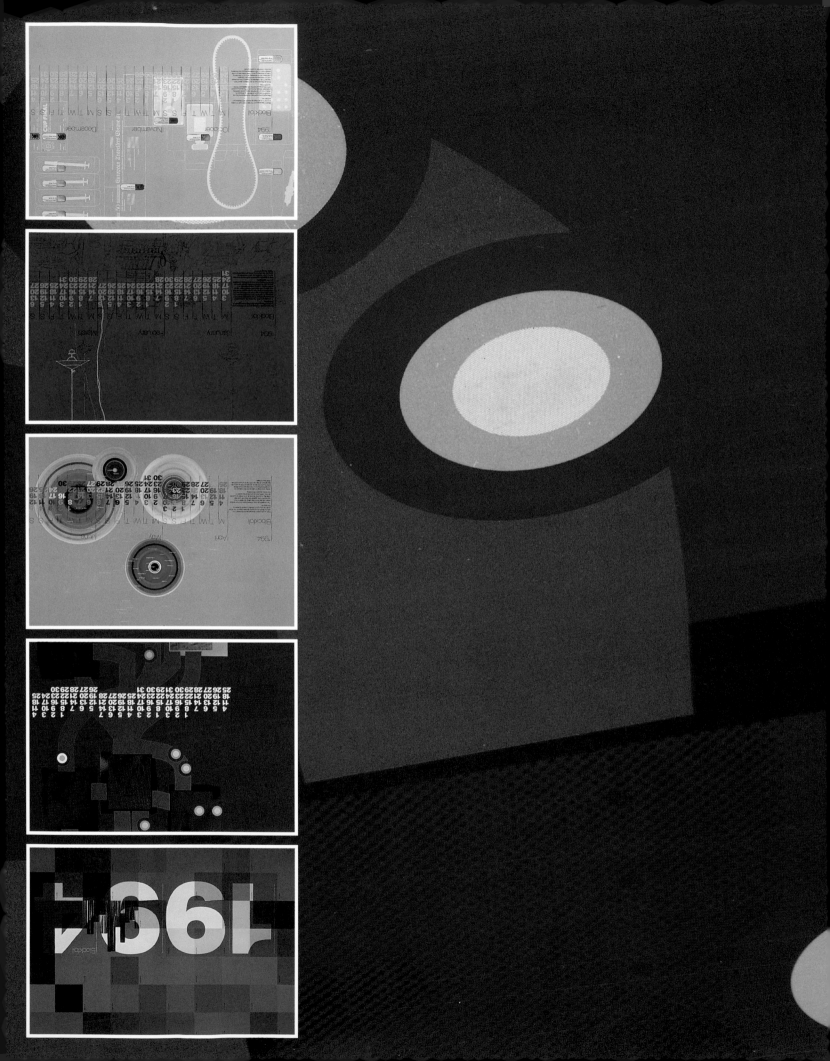

CLIENT
BLOCKFOIL (IPSWICH) LTD

PROJECT TITLE
BLOCKFOIL CALENDAR

DESIGN COMPANY
GRAPHIC THOUGHT FACILITY

ILLUSTRATION
LUCINDA ROGERS

DESIGNERS
PAUL NEALE
ANDREW STEVENS

PHOTOGRAPHY
DAVID HARRISON
GTF

P 166 AND 167

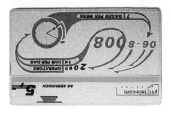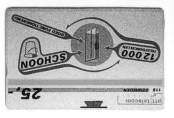

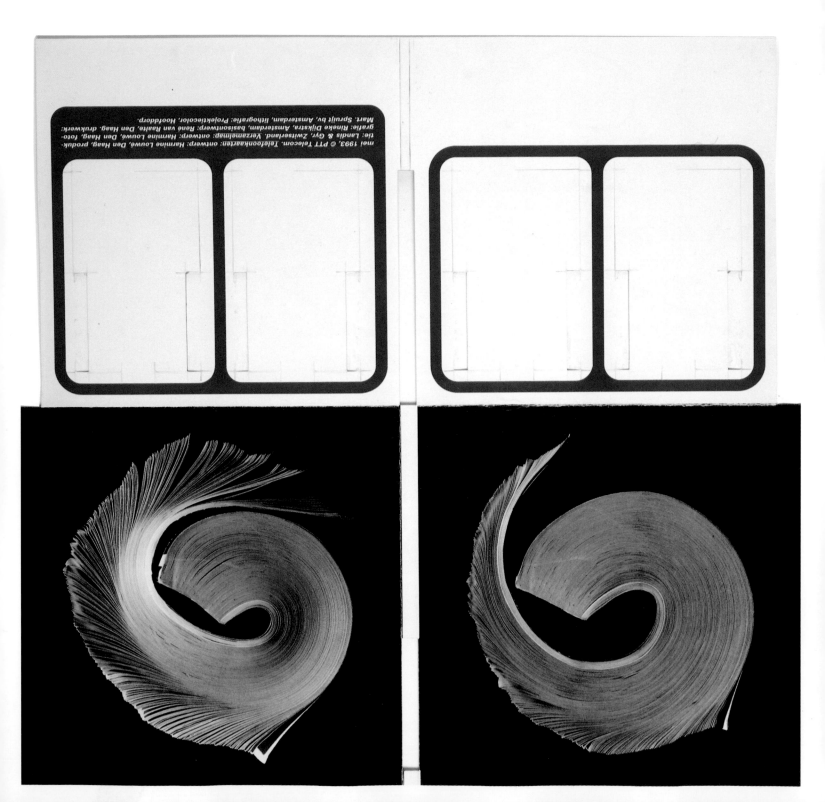

mei 1993. © PTT Telecom. Telefoonkaarten: ontwerp: Harmine Louwe, Den Haag, produk-
tie: Landis & Gyr, Zwitserland. Verzamelmap: ontwerp: Harmine Louwe, Den Haag, foto-
grafie: Rineke Dijkstra, Amsterdam, basisontwerp: René van Raalte, Den Haag, drukwerk:
Mart. Spruijt bv, Amsterdam, lithografie: Projektiecolor, Hoofddorp.

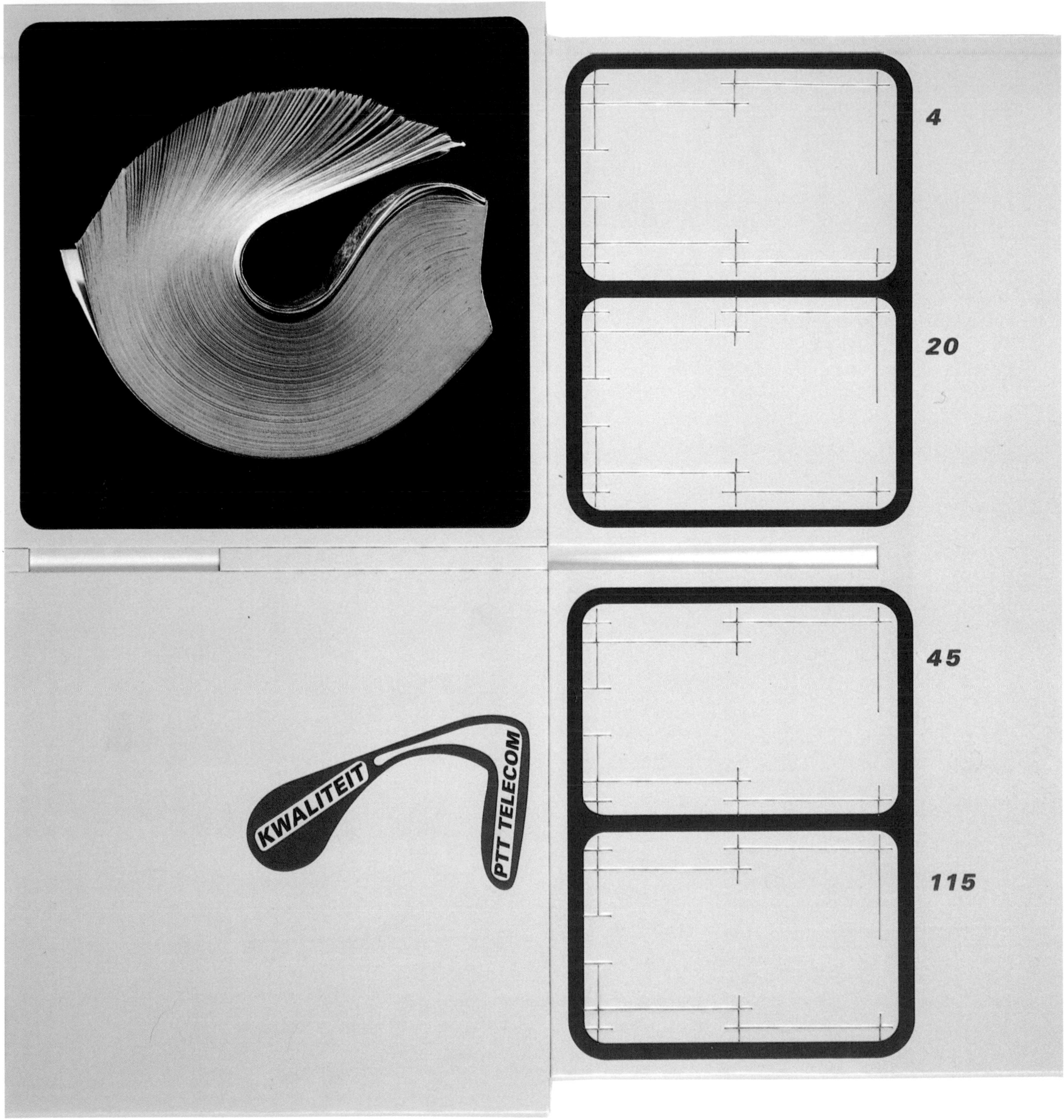

CLIENT	PROJECT TITLE	DESIGNER	PROJECT DESCRIPTION
PTT TELECOM HOLLAND	PTT TELECOM AND SERVICE QUALITY	HARMINE LOUWE PHOTOGRAPHY RINEKE DIJKSTRA	PHONE CARDS AND WALLET 1992 – 1993

P 168 AND 169

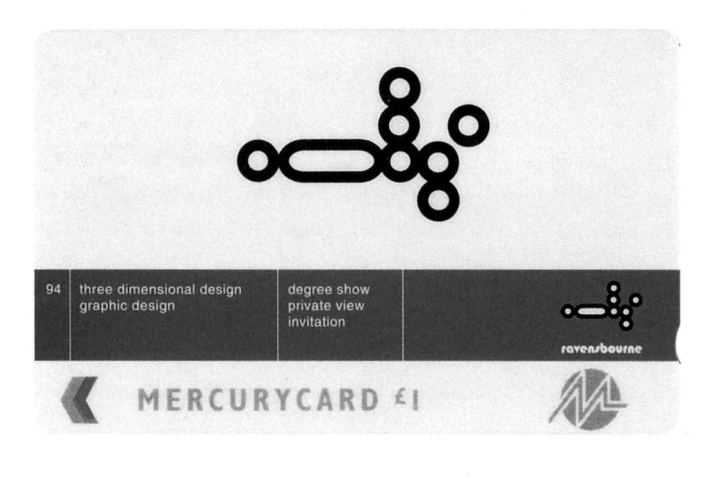

94 | three dimensional design | degree show
graphic design | private view
| invitation

ravensbourne

MERCURYCARD £1

49MERDNEA001558

0.1	date	11.07.94
0.2	start	18.00
0.3	finish	21.00
0.4	information	**tuc congress house**
		great russell street
		london wc1b 3ls

CLIENT
RAVENSBOURNE COLLEGE OF
DESIGN AND COMMUNICATION

DESIGN COMPANY
003

DESIGNERS
NX 44 83 81 NM
NX 74 51 15 UP

PROJECT DESCRIPTION
AN INVITATION TO A PRIVATE VIEW OF AN EXHIBITION, IN THE FORM OF
A WORKING PHONE CARD, ON THE THEME OF DIVERSITY OF LANGUAGE
AND FORM

P 170 AND 171

A WORK FOR THE NORTH SEA

WHERE THE LAND MEETS THE SEA, 8 BULGARIAN WOMEN SING THEIR HAUNTING MELODIES ACROSS THE SEA.

ARTISTS
BETHAN HUWS
THE BISTRITSA BABI

PROJECT TITLE
A WORK FOR THE NORTH SEA
1993

COMMISSIONING ORGANISATION
THE ARTANGEL TRUST

PHOTOGRAPHY
I JEDRZEJCZYK
LISA HARTY

P 172 AND 173

ARTIST	TITLE		CAPTIONS	PROJECT DESCRIPTION
DAMIEN HIRST	IN AND OUT OF LOVE		1	1 DETAIL – GLOSS HOUSEHOLD PAINT ON CANVAS AND BUTTERFLY
	1991		2	2 WHITE PAINTINGS AND LIVE BUTTERFLIES

FIVE WHITE CANVASES WITH PUPAE, STEEL SHELVES WITH POTTED FLOWERS, BOWLS OF SUGAR-WATER SOLUTION, TABLE, RADIATORS, HUMIDIFIERS AND LIVE BUTTERFLIES.

STANSTED, LONDON'S THIRD AIRPORT, WILL BE EXPERIENCED BY 15 MILLION AIR TRAVELLERS A YEAR BY THE END OF THE CENTURY.

CLIENT	ARCHITECT	PROJECT DESCRIPTION
BRITISH AIRPORTS AUTHORITY PLC STANSTED AIRPORT	SIR NORMAN FOSTER AND PARTNERS	INTERNATIONAL TERMINAL, LONDON'S THIRD AIRPORT, STANSTED, COMPLETED 1991

P 176 AND 177

SWAMP CREATURE

9 GLASS S

CLIENT
BRITISH AIRPORTS AUTHORITY PLC

COMMISSIONING COMPANY
PUBLIC ART DEVELOPMENT TRUST FOR
BAA PLC'S ART PROGRAMME AT
HEATHROW AIRPORT

PROJECT DESCRIPTION
INSTALLATIONS BY THREE IRISH ARTISTS FOR PIER 4A LINKS, TERMINAL 1

P 178 AND 179 (180 AND 181, 182 AND 183, 184 OVERLEAF)

CAPTIONS

3

2

CAPTIONS

1

ARTIST MAURICE O'CONNELL

PROJECT TITLE 1, 2, 3 SOUND INSTALLATION

PHOTOGRAPHY JOHN BUTLER

CAPTIONS

2

3

ARTIST
MICK O'KELLY

CAPTIONS

1

PROJECT TITLE
1, 2, 3 PHOTOGRAPHY INSTALLATION
GENUS

PHOTOGRAPHY
PORTRAITS/MICK O'KELLY
INSTALLATION/JOHN BUTLER

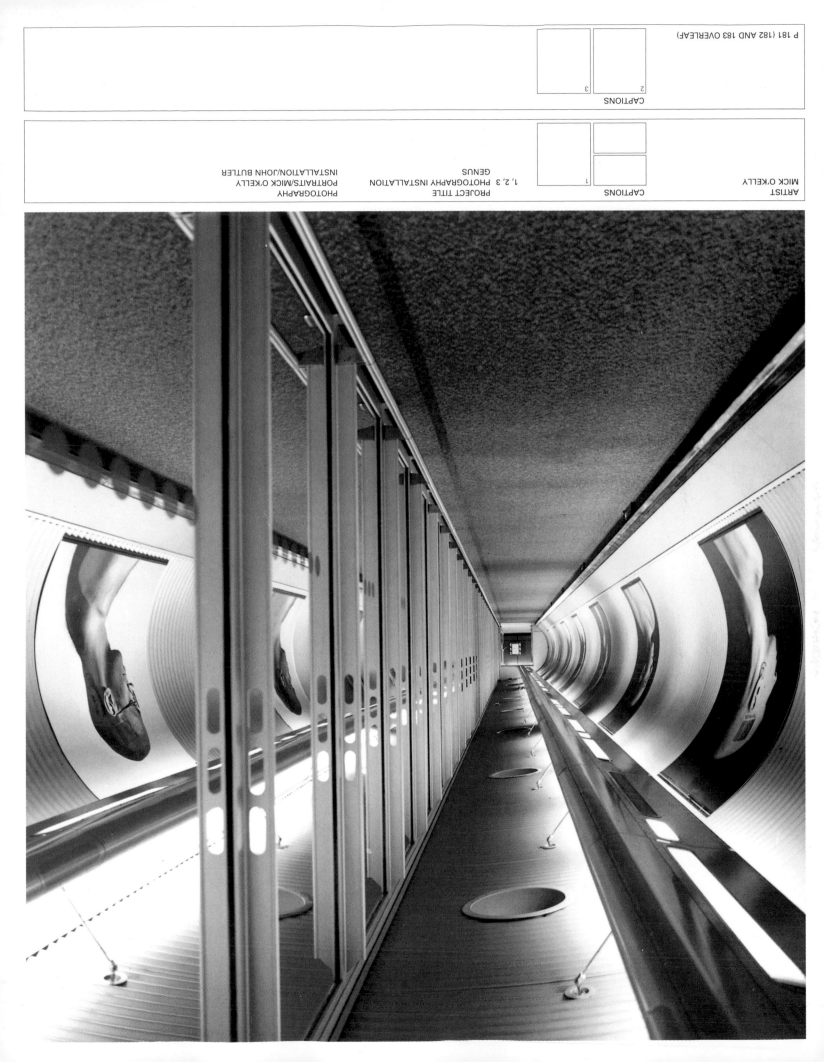

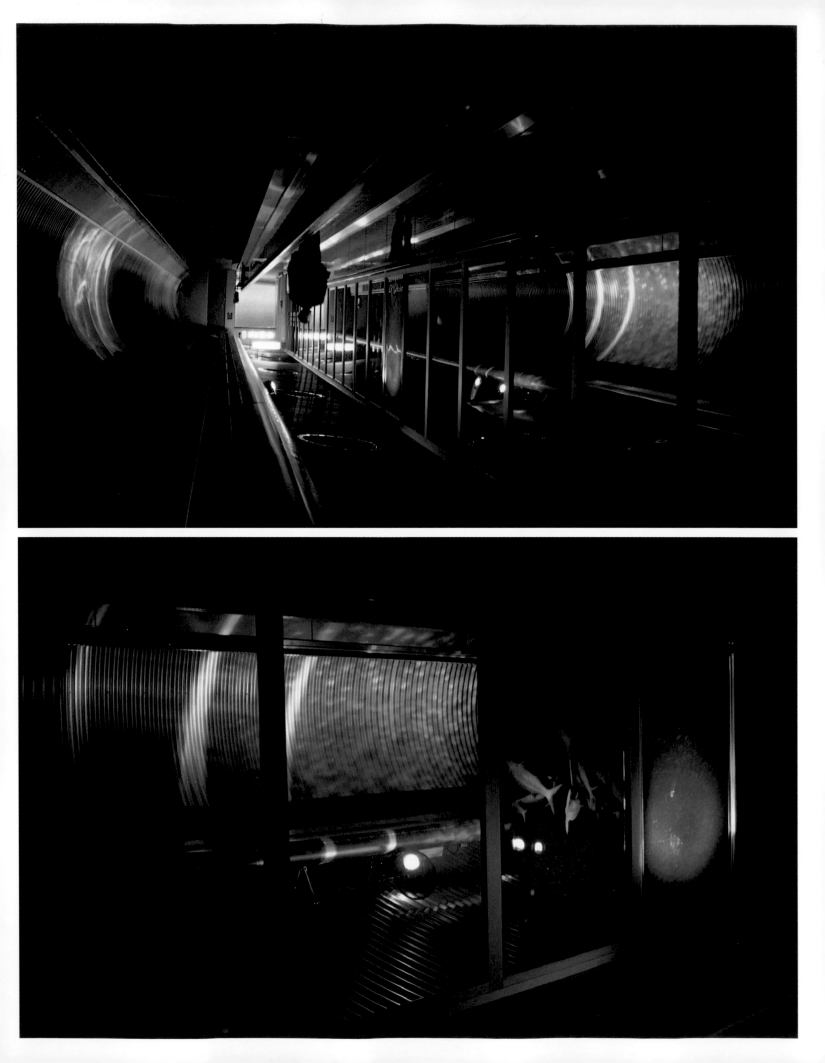

ARTIST
LOUISE WALSH

CAPTIONS 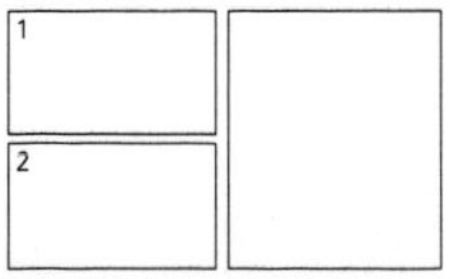
1

2

PROJECT TITLE
1, 2   LIGHT INSTALLATION

PHOTOGRAPHY
PAUL KAY
INSTALLATION/JOHN BUTLER

P 184

THE TRANSLUCENT MEMBRANE HAS LIGHT, COLOUR AND IMAGERY CAST ONTO IT FROM THE OUTSIDE, TO BE VIEWED BY CUSTOMERS AS THEY JOURNEY ALONG THE WALKWAY FROM THE EXISTING STORE INTO THE NEW DEPARTMENT.

CLIENT
HMV UK LTD

PROJECT TITLE
HMV GAMES 'LEVEL ONE'

DESIGN COMPANY
RED JACKET

PHOTOGRAPHY
CHRIS GASCOIGNE

PROJECT DESCRIPTION
COMPUTER GAMES
DEPARTMENT 1993

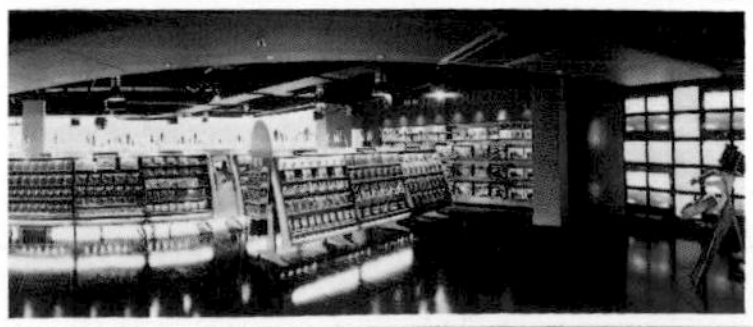

P 186 AND 187

CLIENT
UNITED PUBLISHERS S.A

PROJECT TITLE
VIEW ON COLOUR
NOS 2, 3 AND 4

DESIGN COMPANY
STUDIO ANTHON BEEKE
STUDIO LIDEWIJ EDELKOORT

DESIGNER
ANTHON BEEKE

PROJECT DESCRIPTION
COLOUR FORECASTING MAGAZINE

P 188 AND 189 (190 AND 191, 192 AND 193 OVERLEAF)

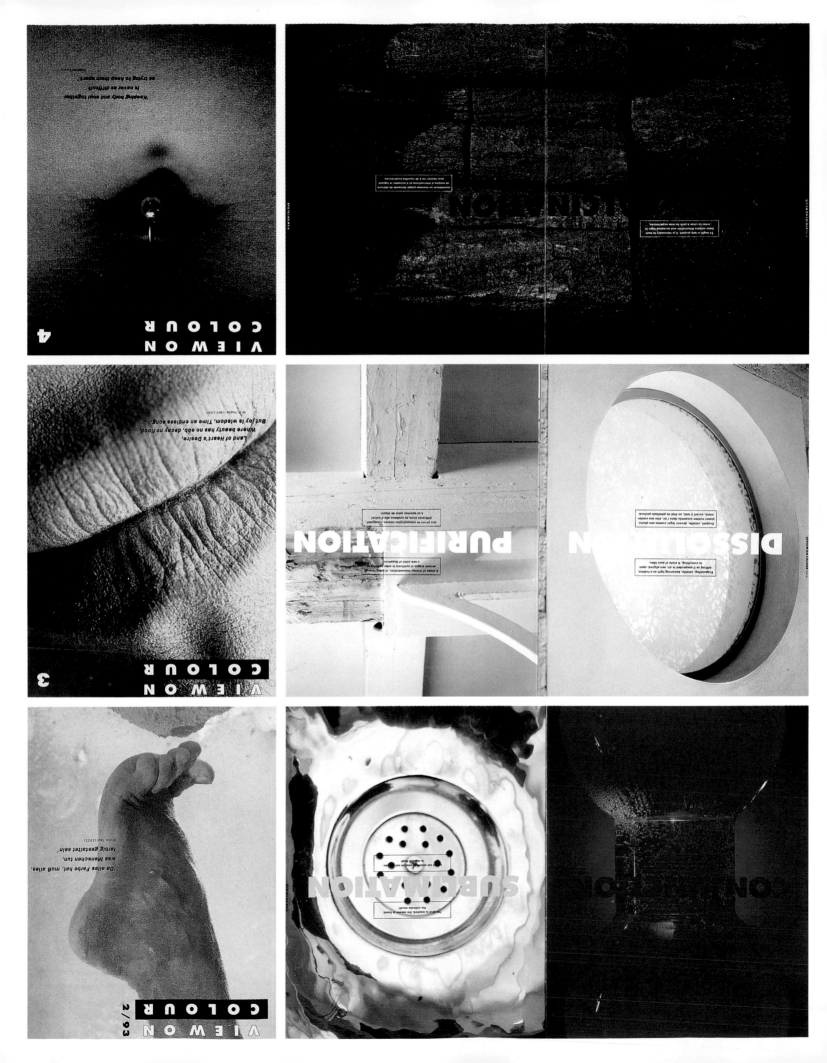

'VIEW ON COLOUR'S AIM IS TO TALK COLOUR TO COLOUR USERS. IT IS DEDICATED TO ALL AREAS THAT NEED TO KNOW WHAT IS HAPPENING IN AND AROUND COLOUR: TEXTILES, FASHION, LEISURE, COSMETICS, GRAPHICS, INDUSTRIAL DESIGN, ARCHITECTURE, INTERIOR DESIGN, PACKAGING, HORTICULTURE...'

THE MAGAZINE IS DESIGNED TO
BALANCE PURE TREND INFORMATION
WITH ARTICLES AND INTERVIEWS OF
GENERAL COLOUR INTEREST. THIS IS
DONE BY FORECASTING THE COLOURS
OF TOMORROW, GIVING EXACT COLOUR
GUIDELINES FOR SELECTED INDUSTRIAL
END-USES, DEMONSTRATING HOW
COLOURS CAN BE USED IN NEW WAYS,
SHOWING HOW DIFFERENT FIELDS OF
INDUSTRY USE AND INTERACT WITH
COLOUR, TALKING TO THE PEOPLE THAT
INFLUENCE AND LEAD OUR THOUGHTS
ON COLOUR, CREATING A COMMON
COLOUR LANGUAGE FOR THE FUTURE.'
ANTHON BEEKE, LIDEWIJ EDELKOORT
DAVID SHAH

VIEW ON COLOUR

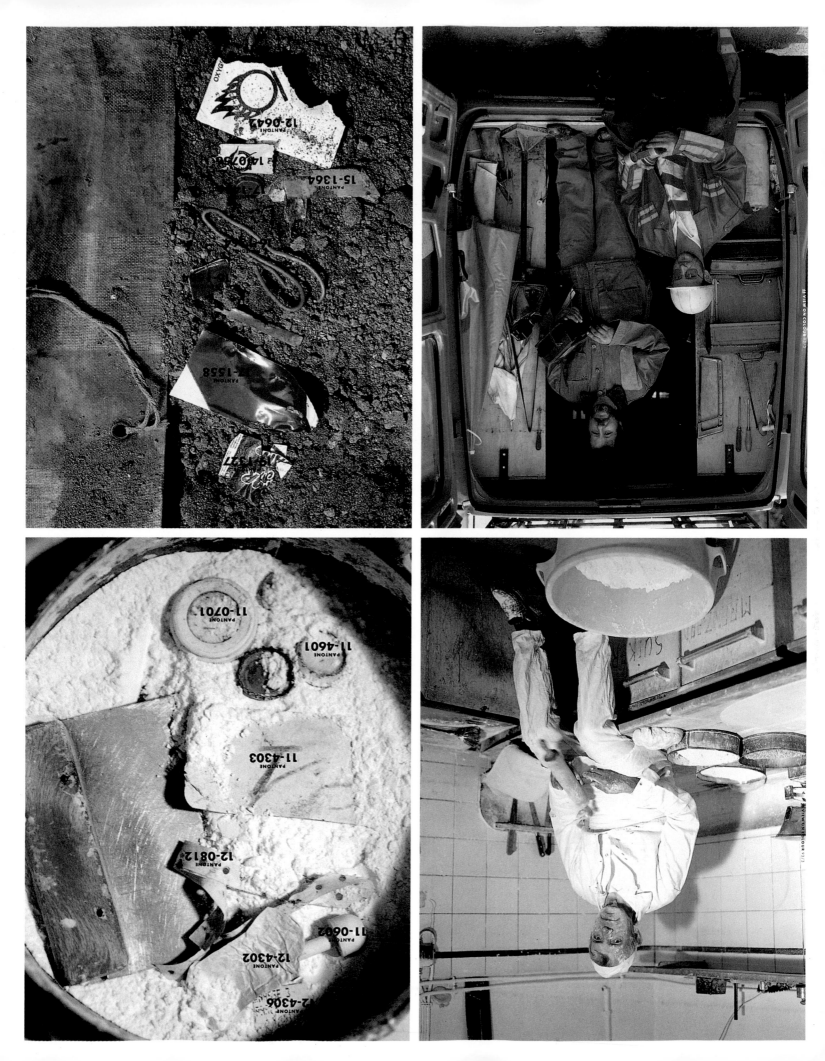

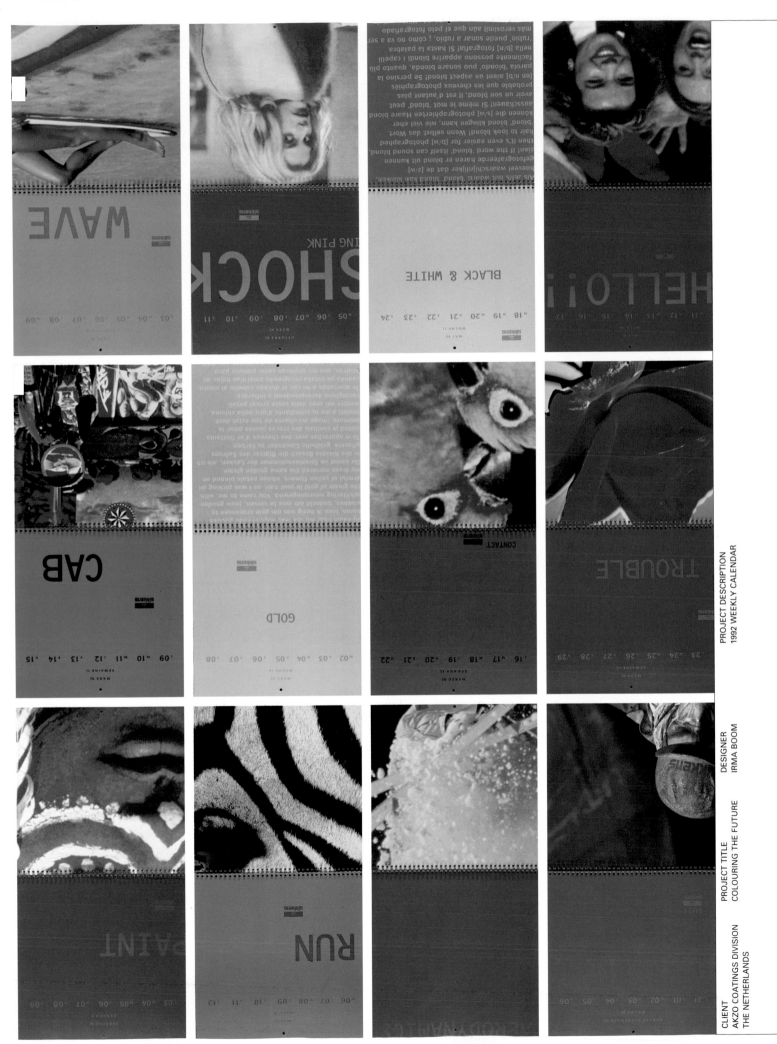

CLIENT
AKZO COATINGS DIVISION
THE NETHERLANDS

PROJECT TITLE
COLOURING THE FUTURE

DESIGNER
IRMA BOOM

PROJECT DESCRIPTION
1992 WEEKLY CALENDAR

P 194 AND 195

PRODUCT MANUFACTURER BECOMES PUBLISHER TO CREATE A CONSUMER LIFESTYLE MAGAZINE DEDICATED TO THE SONY BRAND.

IT CONTAINS FEATURES AND ARTICLES RELATING TO SONY PRODUCTS, RELEVANT LIFESTYLE COMMENTARY, ADVERTISING FROM ALL SONY INDUSTRIES, PRODUCT LISTINGS, PRICES AND INFORMATION.

MAGAZINE AVAILABLE AT NEWS-STANDS OR BY PHONE ORDER.

COMPANY	PROJECT TITLE	ARCHITECT	PROJECT DESCRIPTION
SONY	SONY TOWER	KISHO KUROKAWA	SONY HAVE BUILT SEVERAL SONY CENTRES IN JAPAN AND, MORE
			RECENTLY, IN THE US AND EUROPE. THESE INTERACTIVE AND ENGAG-
			ING SPACES PROVIDE A THREE-DIMENSIONAL REPRESENTATION OF THE
			SONY BRAND WITHIN WHICH THE VISITOR MAY EXPERIENCE THE SONY
P 198 AND 199			'STORY' AND VISIT PRODUCT SHOWROOMS, MUSEUMS, BOOKSHOPS
			EXHIBITS AND CINEMAS

COMPANY	PROJECT TITLE	PROJECT DESCRIPTION
SONY CORPORATION OF AMERICA	SONY STYLE MAGAZINE	THE VALUES AND PERSONALITY OF THE SONY BRAND HAVE ALSO BEEN
		SUCCESSFULLY EMBODIED IN SONY STYLE. HERE THE TRADITIONAL
		PRODUCT CATALOGUE IS 'DIMENSIONALISED' TO EMBRACE LIFESTYLE
		ISSUES, TRENDS AND OPINIONS. IT PROVIDES THE CONSUMER WITH A
		VALUABLE BRAND 'COMPANION' AND THE SONY CORPORATION WITH
P 196 AND 197 (PREVIOUS)		AN INNOVATIVE MARKET ENTRY AND NEW BUSINESS OPPORTUNITY

'THE MINUTE YOU OR ANYBODY ELSE KNOWS WHAT YOU ARE YOU ARE NOT IT. YOU ARE WHAT YOU OR ANYBODY ELSE KNOWS YOU ARE AND AS EVERYTHING IN LIVING IS MADE UP OF FINDING OUT WHAT YOU ARE IT IS EXTRAORDINARILY DIFFICULT REALLY NOT TO KNOW WHAT YOU ARE AND YET TO BE THAT THING.'

GERTRUDE STEIN

P 200 AND 201 (202 AND 203 OVERLEAF)

CLIENT	DESIGN COMPANY	DESIGNERS	PHOTOGRAPHY	PROJECT DESCRIPTION
DECONSTRUCTION	FARROW	ROB PETRIE MARK FARROW PHIL SIMS	ELLEN VON UNWERTH KATRINA JEBB	THE 'RE-ENGINEERING' OF KYLIE MINOGUE

KYLIE MINOGUE

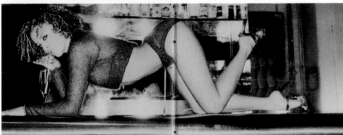

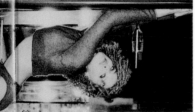
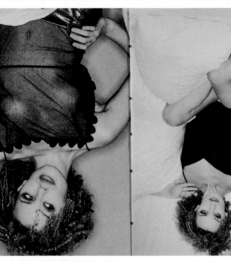

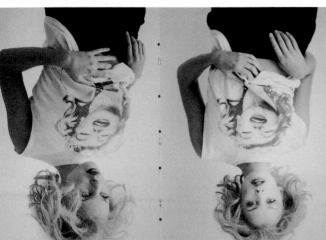

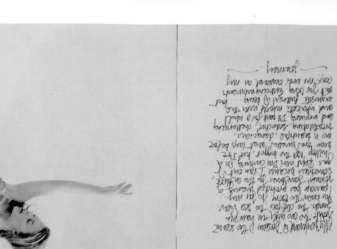

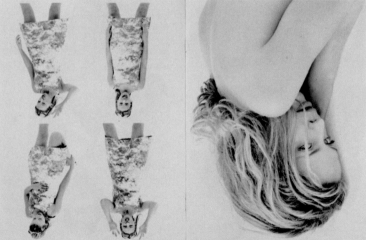
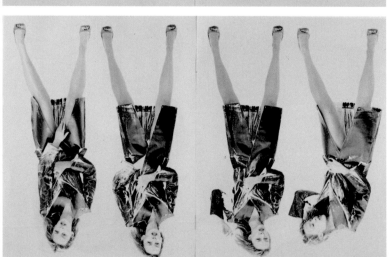

PUBLISHER
ANOTHER LTD

PROJECT TITLE
THE KYLIE BIBLE

MAGAZINE
DAZED AND CONFUSED
1994

STYLING
KATIE GRAND

HAIR AND MAKE UP
SHARON IVES

PROJECT DESCRIPTION
THE 'RE-ENGINEERING' OF KYLIE MINOGUE

PHOTOGRAPHY
RANKIN

P 204 AND 205

THE KYLIE BIBLE

OUTPOST IS A COLLECTABLE EXHIBITION WHICH IN 1994 INCLUDED OVER 25,000 ARTWORKS BY 250 PRACTITIONERS FROM A MULTITUDE OF DISCIPLINES.

THESE ARTWORKS WERE DISPENSED FREE OF CHARGE FROM VENDING BOXES SITUATED IN LOCATIONS AS DIVERSE AS ART GALLERIES AND FAST FOOD RESTAURANTS DURING THE EDINBURGH FESTIVAL.

THE VIEWER IS ENCOURAGED TO MAKE THEIR OWN CRITICAL DECISIONS ABOUT ART – ASIDE FROM THOSE IMPOSED ON THEM BY THE GALLERY SYSTEM AND AWAY FROM THE COMMERCIAL VALUE GIVEN TO WORKS OF ART THROUGH EVIDENCE OF AUTHORSHIP.

MOST IMPORTANTLY, OUTPOST ENCOURAGES THE VIEWER TO SIMULTANEOUSLY TAKE ON THE ROLE OF CURATOR, CRITIC AND COLLECTOR.

CLIENT	COMMISSIONING ORGANISATION	ARTIST	PROJECT DESCRIPTION
EDINBURGH FESTIVAL	FAT	JACQUI PANNELL	THIS IS AN ANATOMICAL INVESTIGATION MAPPING THE BODY THROUGH THE DESCRIPTION OF ITS INDIVIDUAL COMPONENT PARTS. CHILDHOOD MEMORY IS EXPLORED THROUGH THE DOCUMENTATION OF PHYSICAL INCIDENT, USING THE PLASTER AS A COMMON SIGNIFIER OF INJURY. THE WORK ENCOURAGES SIMILAR MEMORIES WITHIN THE VIEWER AND FORCES AN EXPLORATION OF THE CONSTRUCTION OF THEIR OWN IDENTITY
	PROJECT TITLE OUTPOST	CARD TITLE A HUNDRED AND ONE WOUNDS	

| | | ARTIST HELEN CHADWICK | PROJECT DESCRIPTION THESE CARDS DEAL WITH THE NOTION OF EXCHANGE. THE VIEWER RECEIVES THE DONEE CARD IN RETURN FOR THE DONATION OF A PINT OF BLOOD. THE ARTIST REQUIRED THE TERMS OF EXCHANGE TO BE OF EQUAL BENEFIT TO ALL PARTIES INVOLVED – THE VIEWER RECEIVES A VALUABLE PIECE OF WORK, SOCIETY BENEFITS FROM THE DONATION OF VITAL FLUID – AND THE ARTIST BENEFITS FROM THE KNOWLEDGE OF THIS EXCHANGE |
| | | CARD TITLE DONOR/DONEE | |

| | | ARTIST MIKE NELSON | PROJECT DESCRIPTION THIS WORK EMPOWERS THE VIEWER WITH A PHYSICAL MEANS OF ENGAGEMENT – ARSON – WITHIN THE CONTEXT THAT THE WORK IS EXPERIENCED. THE MANIFESTATION OF THIS ENGAGEMENT IS CONDITIONED BY THE VIEWER'S RELATIONSHIP TO THE INSTITUTION WHICH THEY OCCUPY |
| | | CARD TITLE ARSON | |

P 207

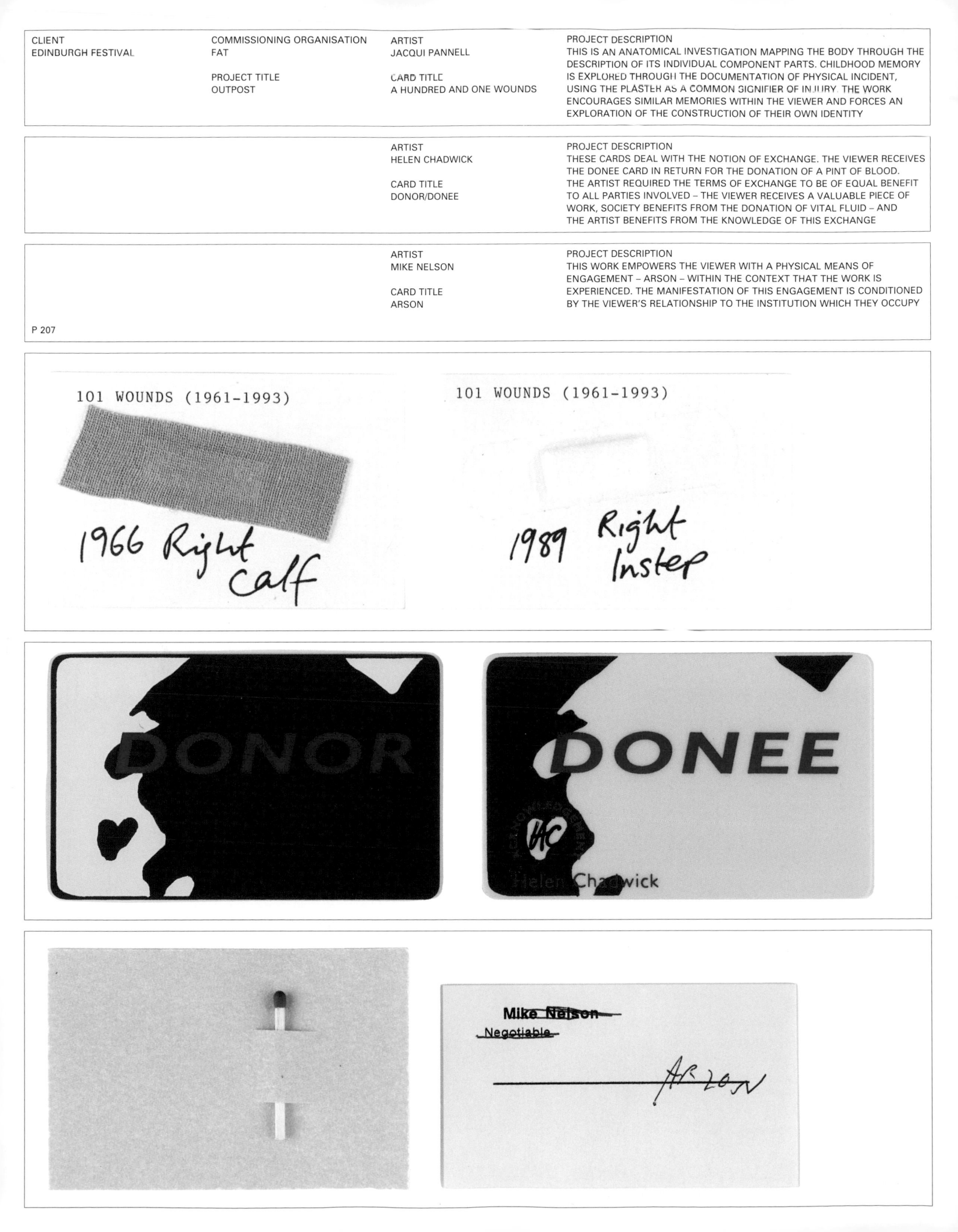

CLIENT EDINBURGH FESTIVAL	COMMISSIONING ORGANISATION FAT	ARTIST LISA BROWN	PROJECT DESCRIPTION THIS WORK EXPOSES AN OFTEN PRIVATE FEMALE RITUAL THROUGH THE DISTRIBUTION OF DISCARDED HAIR WAXING STRIPS WHICH PREVIOUSLY RENDERED THE BODY 'PERFECT'. THE VIEWER IS OFFERED THE OPPORTUNITY
	PROJECT TITLE OUTPOST	CARD TITLE PERFECT BESTIALITY	TO CHALLENGE AND RECONSTRUCT THEIR OWN IDEALS OF FEMALE 'PERFECTION' WHEN DECIDING WHETHER TO UTILISE THE UNUSED WAX OF THE SIGNATURE CARD

		ARTIST PIP BRUCE	PROJECT DESCRIPTION WHEN THE ENVELOPE IS OPENED THE PARTIALLY DEVELOPED PHOTOGRAPH CONTAINED WITHIN CONTINUES TO EXPOSE. THIS PROCESS CAN ONLY BE HALTED BY THE VIEWER PLACING THE WORK IMMEDIATELY BACK WITHIN ITS
		CARD TITLE POSSESSION	COVERING. THE WORK INVITES THE SPECTATOR TO ENGAGE IN IDEAS OF POSSESSION AND PERMANENCE BY OFFERING THEM THE CHOICE OF EITHER MOMENTARILY EXPERIENCING THE IMAGE, OR PRESERVING IT UNSEEN

		ARTIST STAN O	PROJECT DESCRIPTION EACH URINE FILLED SACHET WAS LOCATED WITHIN MAJOR INSTITUTIONS THROUGHOUT THE CITY, MARKING OUT THE TERRITORY OCCUPIED AND ENGAGED BY THE ARTIST. THE SIGNATURE CARD TAKES THE FORM OF THE
P 208		CARD TITLE PISS MARK	LAMINATED FRAGMENT OF A GLOVE WHICH ENABLED THE ARTIST TO MAKE THE WORK AND ENABLES THE VIEWER TO 'TOUCH' AND SYMBOLICALLY 'OWN' THE WORK

ARTIST
THOMAS TATUM

CARD TITLE
PURE

PROJECT DESCRIPTION
ONE HALF OF A CHEQUE IS 'BROUGHT' WITH THE OTHER HALF, HIGHLIGHTING THE LACK OF REAL COMMERCIAL VALUE IN ART AND REDUCING ARTWORK TO A PURE TRANSACTION OF PRODUCT. IN FILLING OUT THE CHEQUE THE VIEWER QUESTIONS AND DETERMINES THE VALUE OF THE ARTWORK THEMSELVES – THEY DECIDE IN MONEY TERMS, HOW MUCH THE WORK IS WORTH TO THEM AND HOW MUCH THEY ARE WILLING TO PAY

ARTIST
EMMA DAVIS
CLIVE SALL

CARD TITLE
RED CROSS

PROJECT DESCRIPTION
THIS WORK ENGAGES WITH A NOTION OF HEALING WHICH OCCURS ON TWO LEVELS. FIRSTLY, THE REPRESENTATION OF THE ILLNESS IS CUT AWAY IN ORDER TO CURE THE AILING BODY – THE ARTIST ACTS AS SURGEON AND HEALER TO THE AFFLICTED OCCUPIER OF THE IMAGE. SECONDLY THE VIEWER IS 'HEALED' THROUGH THE AESTHETIC OF THE 'ILLNESS' ITSELF WHILST INVESTIGATING IT AS AN INDEPENDENT IMAGE OF TEXTURE AND COLOUR

ARTIST
FRANCOIS LE FRANC

CARD TITLE
100 NATURAL HOME SETTINGS
SYCAMORE FANTASY

PROJECT DESCRIPTION
THE 100 FORMICA WOOD LAMINATED CARDS, APPROPRIATING A CATALOGUE OF SAMPLES, SIGNIFY THE OPPORTUNITY OF A VOLUPTUOUS TOTAL ENVIRONMENT. THE SAMPLES, DESPITE THEIR SIZE, CONSTITUTE A COMPLETE AND IDEAL SET OF CHOICES, OFFERING THE DOMESTIC CONSUMER THE PROMISE OF BOTH NOSTALGIA AND EXPECTATION

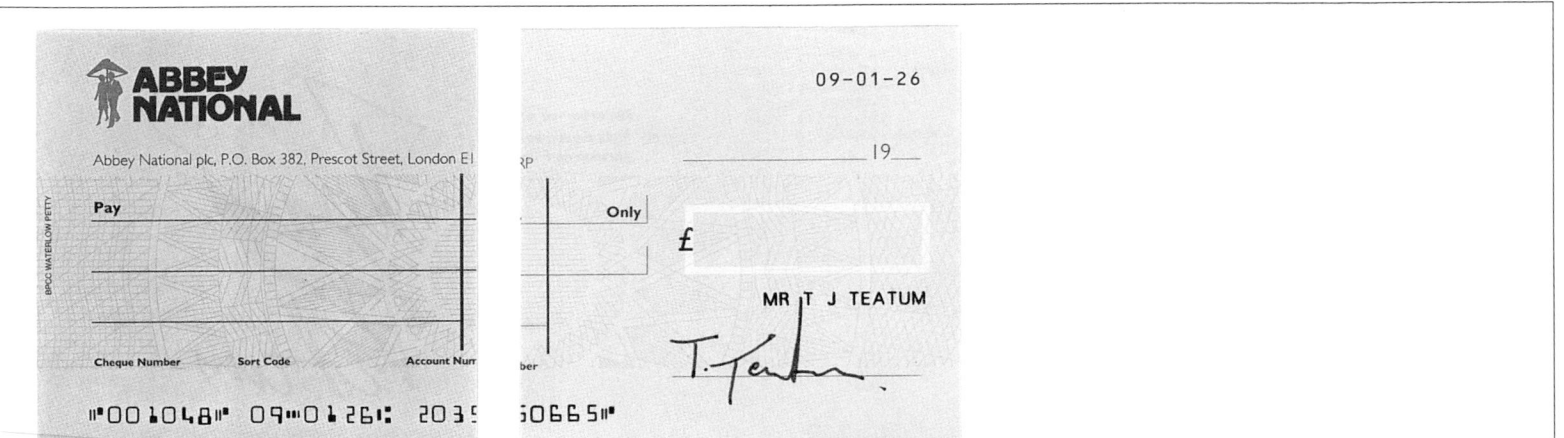

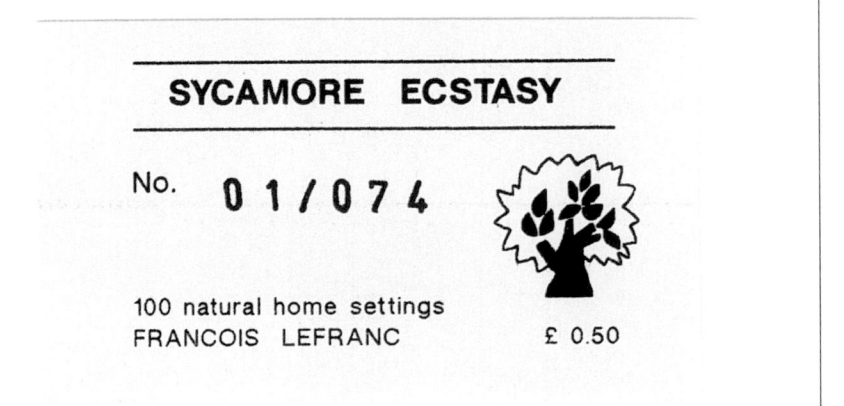

CLIENT	COMMISSIONING ORGANISATION	ARTIST	PROJECT DESCRIPTION
EDINBURGH FESTIVAL	FAT	REBEKAH CAMERON	EACH SACHET CONTAINS THE FRAGMENTS OF ONE HALF OF A PHOTOGRAPH
			– EVIDENCE OF A PERSONAL RELATIONSHIP FROM THE ARTIST'S PAST.
	PROJECT TITLE	CARD TITLE	THE VIEWER IS DRAWN INTO THE CONSTRUCTION OF THE NARRATIVE AND
	OUTPOST	SEPARATED	COMBINESS THE HALVES TO REVEAL THE FULL IMAGE TOGETHER WITH A
			TEXTUAL DESCRIPTION

	ARTIST	PROJECT DESCRIPTION
	TERRY HAGERTY	THE SEALED ENVELOPE INVITES THE INVESTIGATION OF ITS CONTENTS.
		UPON OPENING THE PIGMENT IT CONTAINS IS TRANSFERRED TO THE HANDS
	CARD TITLE	OF THE VIEWER THEREBY IMPLICATING THEM IN THE PROCESS OF IMAGE
	BRY	MAKING. THIS INTERACTIVE ENGAGEMENT ENCOURAGES AN ACTUAL PHYSI-
		CAL EXPERIENCE WITH THE WORK AND ITS MEANS OF PRODUCTION

	ARTIST	PROJECT DESCRIPTION
	JACQUELINE PANNELL	THIS IMAGE INVESTIGATES THE CONCEPTUAL SPACE BETWEEN TWO AND
		THREE-DIMENSIONAL CONDITIONS. THE VIEWER IS ENCOURAGED TO
	CARD TITLE	CONSIDER THE PROCESS OF THE PRODUCTION OF THE WORK THROUGH
	MOMENTS WITH OBJECTS	AN INTER-ACTIVE SPATIAL ENGAGEMENT
	THE PIN	

P 210

Moments With Objects
The Pin

Jacqueline Pennell

ARTIST
ALEXANDRA POWERS

CARD TITLE
SYRUP OF FIGS

PROJECT DESCRIPTION
THE WAY IN WHICH WE PERCEIVE OUR OWN SELF-IMAGE AND HOW IT IS
RE-INVENTED IS EXAMINED BY USE OF THE HAIRSTYLE AS FASHION ICON.
THE SIGNATURE CARD PRESENTS THE INVENTED WORD 'SYRUPTITIOUS'
(A MUTATED FORM OF SURREPTITIOUS) SEWN IN THE ARTISTS OWN HAIR

ARTIST
ALAN OUTRAM

CARD TITLE
STOLEN GOODS

PROJECT DESCRIPTION
ATTACHED TO THE CARDS ARE 100 OBJECTS STOLEN FROM DIFFERENT LOCA-
TIONS. THE IMAGES DEAL WITH CONDITIONS OF OWNERSHIP, MONETARY
VALUE AND POSSESSION. THE CARDS 'VALUE' CHANGES ACCORDING TO
WHERE IT WAS STOLEN FROM, AND WHERE IT WAS RETRIEVED. THE CARDS
ALSO OFFER THE EXPERIENCE OF RECEIVING STOLEN GOODS

ARTIST
EMMA DAVIS
CLIVE SALL

CARD TITLE
RED CROSS

PROJECT DESCRIPTION
THIS WORK ENGAGES WITH A NOTION OF HEALING WHICH OCCURS ON TWO
LEVELS. FIRSTLY, THE REPRESENTATION OF THE ILLNESS IS CUT AWAY IN
ORDER TO CURE THE AILING BODY – THE ARTIST ACTS AS SURGEON AND
HEALER TO THE AFFLICTED OCCUPIER OF THE IMAGE. SECONDLY, THE VIEWER
IS 'HEALED' THROUGH THE AESTHETIC OF THE 'ILLNESS' ITSELF WHILST
INVESTIGATING IT AS AN INDEPENDENT IMAGE OF TEXTURE AND COLOUR

P 211

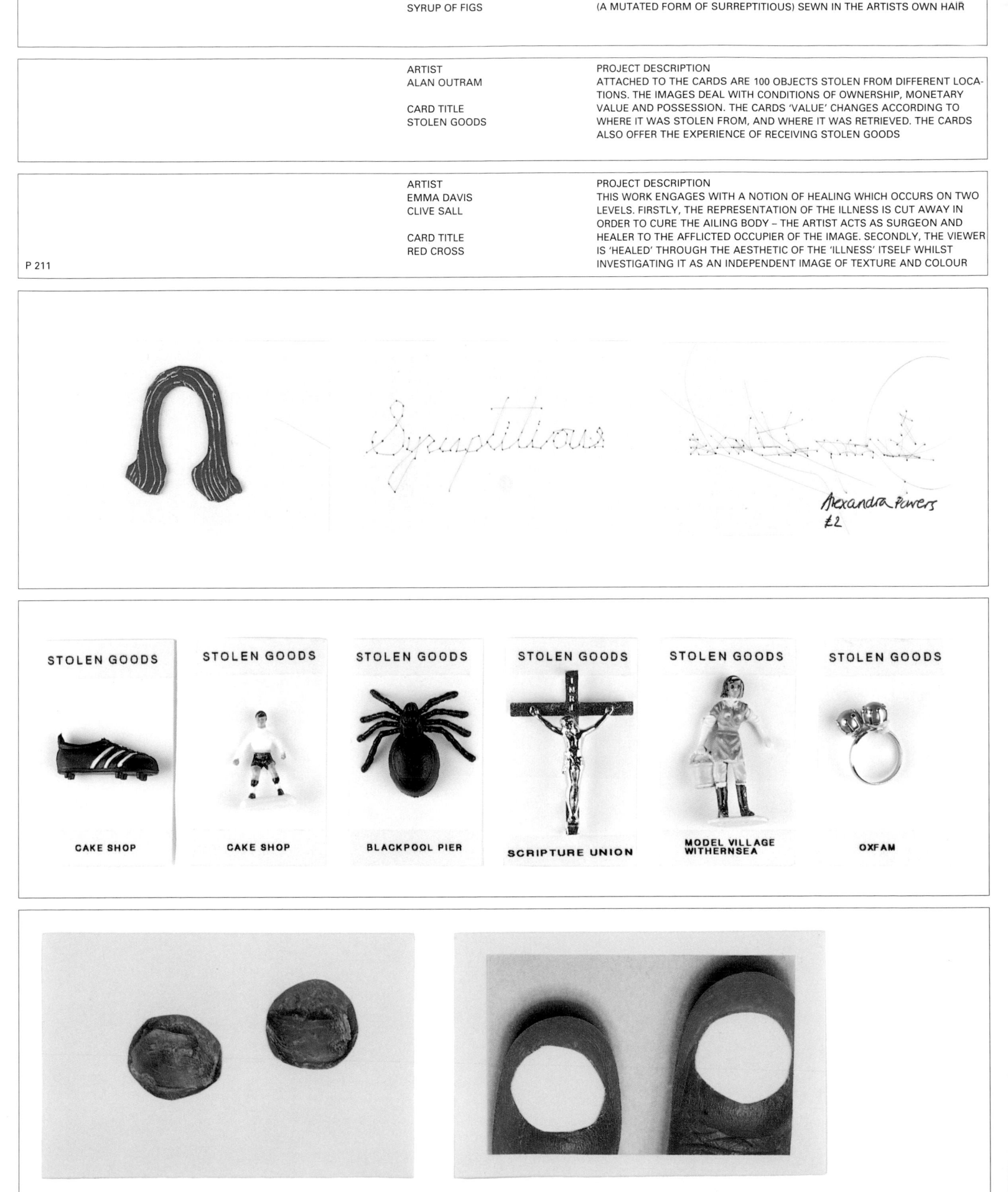

IN THE LATE 19TH CENTURY, GROVE ROAD WAS A TYPICAL ROW OF TERRACE HOUSES OF THE KIND BUILT THROUGH-OUT THE EAST END OF LONDON.

BY THE EARLY 1990'S THE TERRACE WAS NO MORE. FROM THE INTERIOR OF THE LAST REMAINING HOUSE, AN EXTRAORD-INARY SCULPTURE WAS MADE BY THE ARTIST RACHEL WHITEREAD.

THIS WORK COMMEMORATES MEMORY ITSELF THROUGH THE COMMONPLACE OF THE HOME. WHITEREAD'S IN-SITU WORK TRANSFORMS THE SPACE OF THE PRIVATE AND DOMESTIC INTO THE PUBLIC – A MUTE MEMORIAL TO THE SPACES WE HAVE ALL LIVED IN AND EXPERIENCED.

ARTIST
RACHEL WHITEREAD

PROJECT TITLE
HOUSE 1993

COMMISSIONING ORGANISATION
THE ARTANGEL TRUST

PHOTOGRAPHY
EDWARD WOODMAN

P 212 AND 213

PROJECT DESCRIPTION
INTERIOR AND EXTERIOR INFORMATION SYSTEM
1990

Gasflaschenlager

Schutzbereich 5m

Rauchen, Feuer, offenes Licht verboten

Cafeteria

Cafeteria

Unternehmens-
Bereich
Elektronik und
Optik

Leybold AG

Leybold AG

Leybold AG

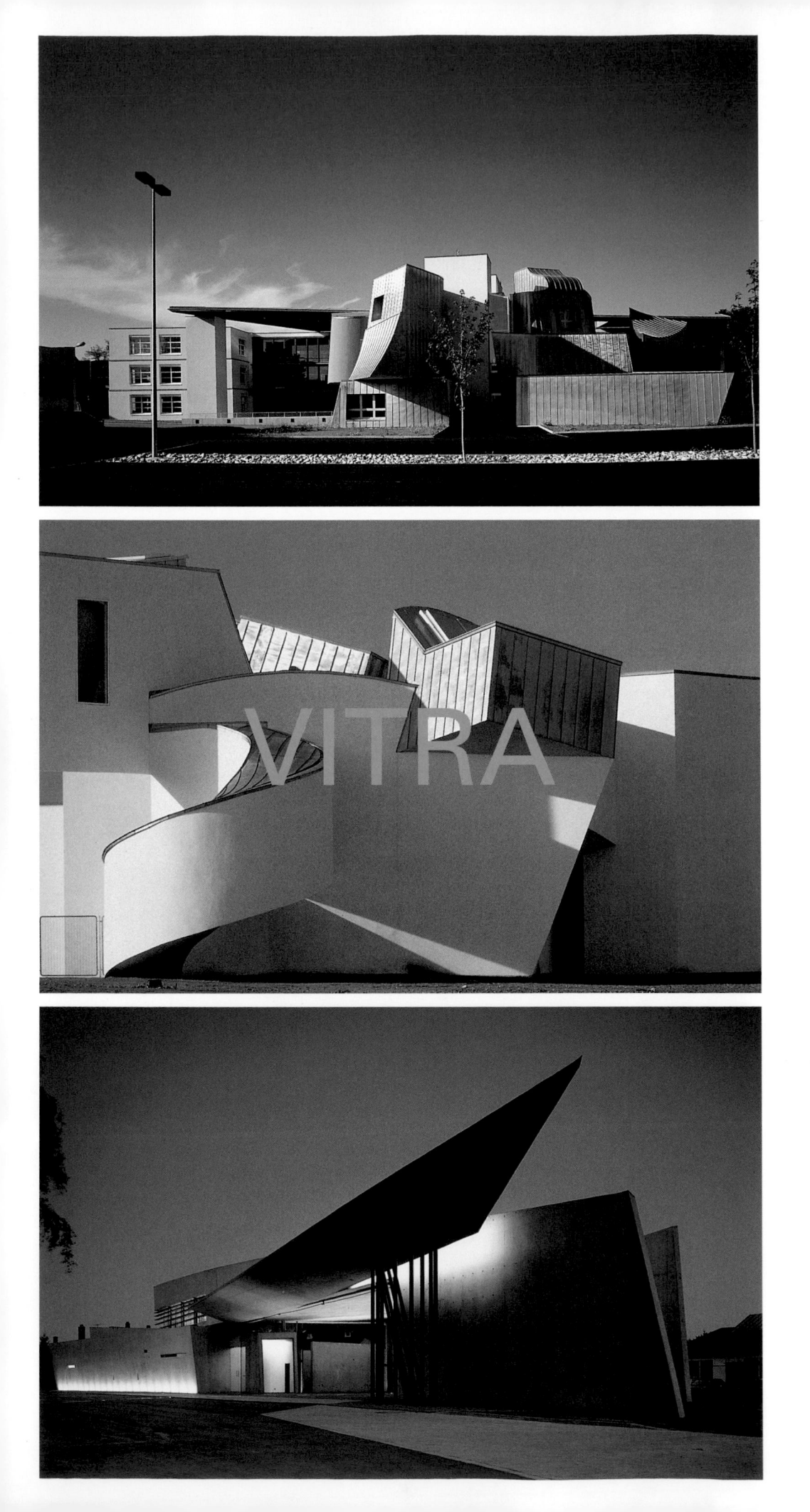

CLIENT	CAPTIONS	PROJECT TITLE	ARCHITECT	PHOTOGRAPHY
VITRA GMBH	1 2 3	1 VITRA CENTRE	FRANK O GEHRY	RICHARD BRYANT
		2 VITRA DESIGN MUSEUM	FRANK O GEHRY	ARCAID
		3 VITRA FIRE STATION	ZAHA M HADID	

'WHEN THE VITRA DESIGN MUSEUM WAS OPENED ON NOVEMBER 3 1989, FRANK GEHRY'S UNCONVENTIONAL ARCHITEC-TURE PROVIDED US WITH A SIGNIFICANT INITIAL ADVANTAGE. THE FACT THAT OUR MUSEUM WAS NOT ONLY GEHRY'S FIRST BUILDING IN EUROPE BUT ALSO THE INAUGURATION OF A NEW PHASE IN THE ARCHITECT'S WORK, DREW VISITORS FROM ALL OVER THE WORLD,'

ALEXANDER VON VEGESACK

STILLNESS

CLIENT	PROJECT TITLE	ARCHITECT	PROJECT DESCRIPTION

CLIENT
VITRA GMBH

PROJECT TITLE
VITRA CONFERENCE CENTRE

ARCHITECT
TADAO ANDO

PHOTOGRAPHY
RICHARD BRYANT

PROJECT DESCRIPTION
'WHEN FIRST VISITING THE SITE, I WAS STRUCK BY THE MOVEMENT THAT
THE FRANK GEHRY DESIGN MUSEUM PROJECTED SO POWERFULLY.
OPPOSITE GEHRY'S ARCHITECTURE OF MOVEMENT I INTRODUCED THE
ELEMENT OF STILLNESS. THIS ARCHITECTURE OF STILLNESS BEGINS TO
ACQUIRE RICH LIFE WHEN THE ELEMENTS OF NATURE – LIGHT AND WIND –
AND THE MOVEMENT OF PEOPLE ARE INTRODUCED WITHIN IT.' TADAO ANDO

'TODAY THE DIFFERENCE BETWEEN A GOOD AND A POOR ARCHITECT IS THAT THE POOR ARCHITECT SUCCUMBS TO EVERY TEMPTATION AND THE GOOD ONE RESISTS IT.'

L WITTGENSTEIN

CLIENT	PROJECT TITLE	ARCHITECT	PHOTOGRAPHY	PROJECT DESCRIPTION
HANS & CAROLINA NEUENDORF	MAJORCA HOUSE	PAWSON SILVESTRIN	RICHARD BRYANT ARCAID	HOLIDAY VILLA FOR A GERMAN ART DEALER. THE LONG NARROW POOL PROJECTS FROM THE TERRACE TOWARDS THE HORIZON ENDING IN A WATERFALL
		ARCHITECTS JOHN PAWSON CLAUDIO SILVESTRIN		
P 220 AND 221				

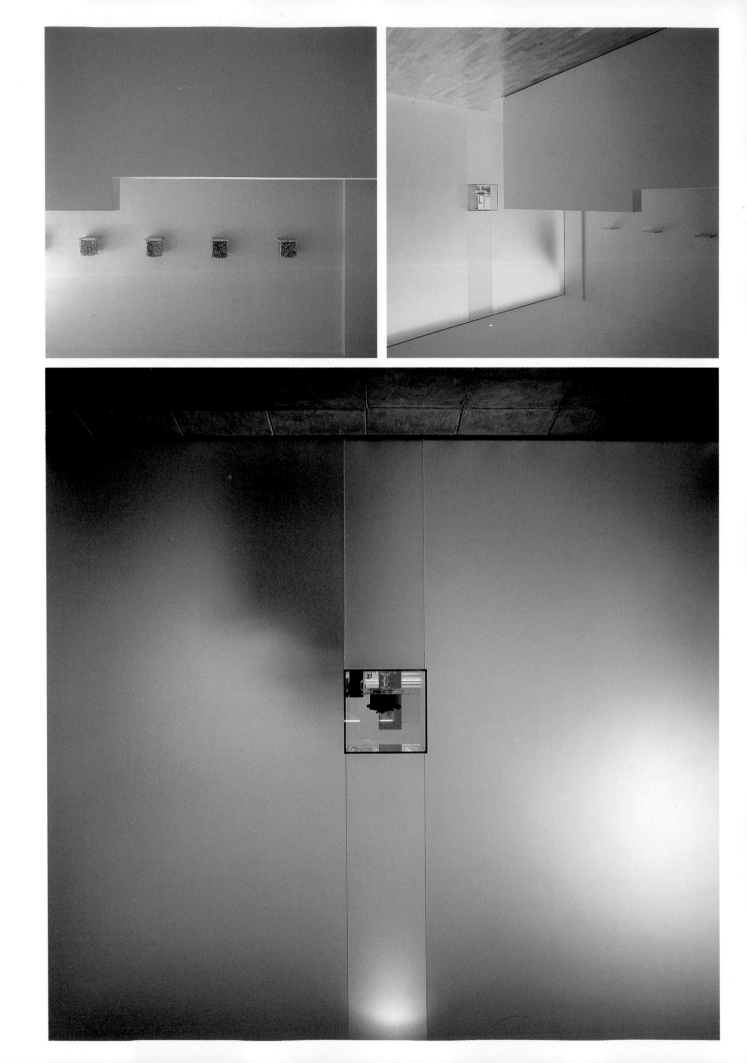

A WALL OF TRANSLUCENT ACID-ETCHED GLASS FORMS THE SHOP FRONT. THIS MASK FACADE IS PUNCTURED BY A CLEAR GLASS CUBE, JUST LARGE ENOUGH FOR THE DISPLAY OF A SINGLE CAKE SET AT ITS CENTRE.

DURING THE DAY THE GLASS FILTERS THE SUNLIGHT IN. AT NIGHT, SEEN FROM OUTSIDE, ARTIFICIAL LIGHT PRODUCES A MYSTERIOUS QUALITY.

CLIENT	PROJECT TITLE	ARCHITECT	PHOTOGRAPHY	PROJECT DESCRIPTION
RAJA CORTAS	CANNELLE	PAWSON SILVESTRIN	IAN DOBBIE	CAKE SHOP INTERIOR AND FACADE
		ARCHITECTS		
		JOHN PAWSON		
		CLAUDIO SILVESTRIN		
P 222 AND 223				

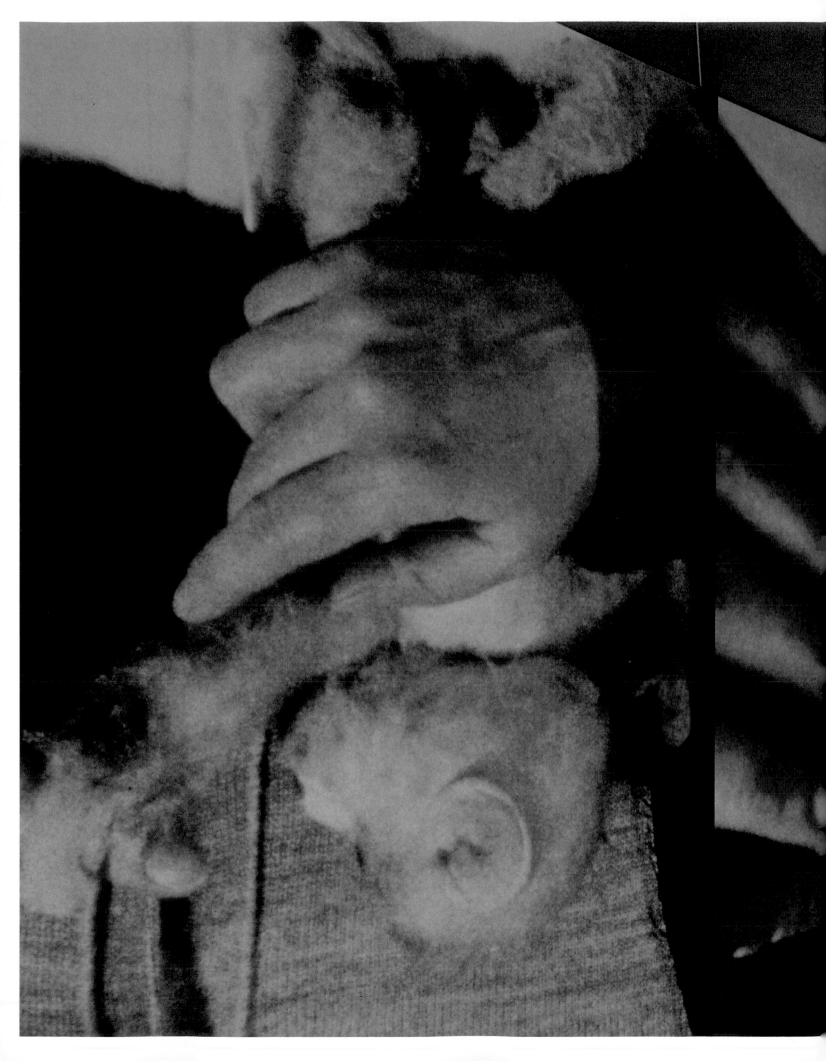

COMPANY
COMME DES GARÇONS

PROJECT
DIRECT MAIL CAMPAIGN

ARTIST
CINDY SHERMAN

PROJECT DESCRIPTION
A SERIES OF 5 CARDS WERE SENT TO COMME DES GARÇONS' CUSTOMERS ANNOUNCING THE AUTUMN/WINTER 1993 – 1994 COLLECTION AND SPRING/SUMMER 1994 COLLECTION

COMME des GARÇONS*

COMME des GARÇONS*

Cindy Sherman © 1993

1993年 秋のコレクションがスタートいたします。どうぞおでかけください。

COMME des GARÇONS

*

COMME des GARÇONS

New selections from our autumn/winter 93-94 collection have arrived.

Cindy Sherman © 1993

COMME des GARÇONS

CLIENT	PROJECT TITLE	DESIGNER	PHOTOGRAPHY	PROJECT DESCRIPTION
REGIS	MOTO	DAVID JAMES	EDDIE MONSOON	FASHION CATALOGUE FOR MANUFACTURER OF PLASTIC AND RUBBER CLOTHING. THE BROCHURE IS MADE OF PLASTIC AND CAN BE SCREWED-UP TO ENABLE ITS CONTENTS TO LITERALLY UNFOLD BEFORE THE VIEWER AND IN DOING SO EXPLOIT THE INTRISIC PHYSICAL PROPERTIES OF THE MATERIALS THEMSELVES

P 232 AND 233 (234 AND 235 OVERLEAF)

'SOME BOOKS ARE TO BE TASTED, OTHERS TO BE SWALLOWED, AND SOME FEW TO BE CHEWED AND DIGESTED.'

FRANCIS BACON

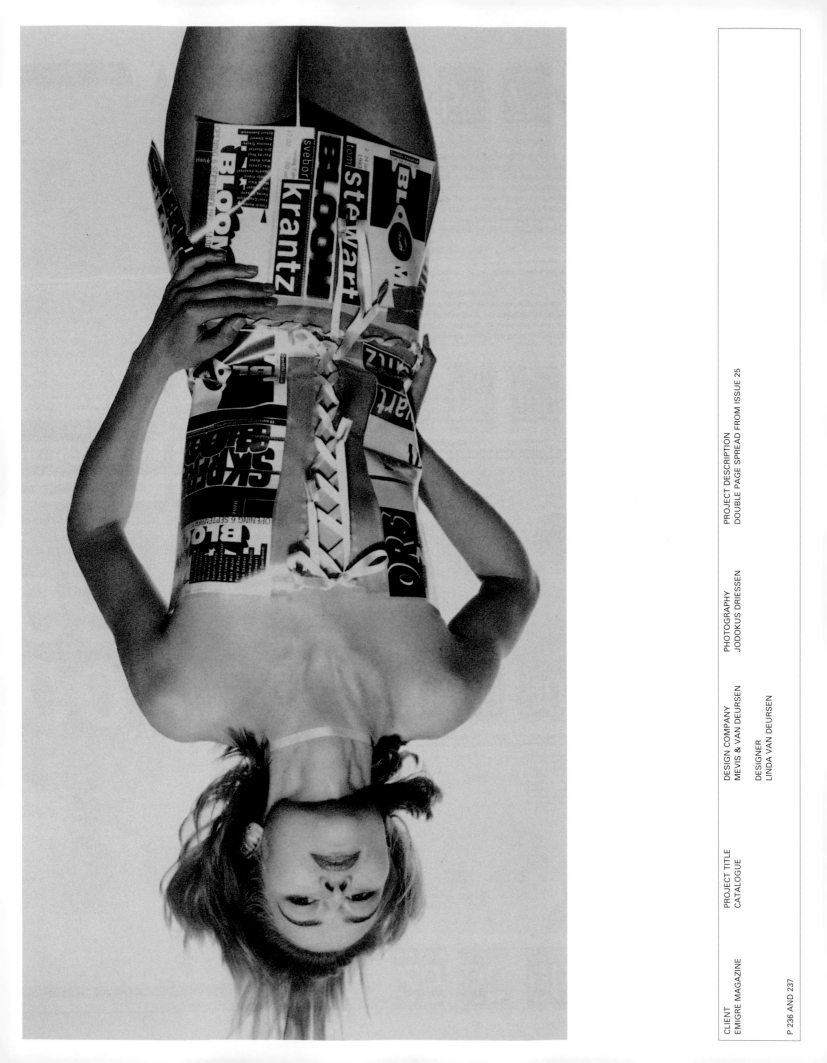

CLIENT
EMIGRE MAGAZINE

PROJECT TITLE
CATALOGUE

DESIGN COMPANY
MEVIS & VAN DEURSEN

DESIGNER
LINDA VAN DEURSEN

PHOTOGRAPHY
JODOKUS DRIESSEN

PROJECT DESCRIPTION
DOUBLE PAGE SPREAD FROM ISSUE 25

P 236 AND 237

A FASHIONABLE PIECE OF LITERATURE

PUBLISHER
FUSE/FONTSHOP INTERNATIONAL

PROJECT TITLE
ANALPHABET 1994

DESIGNER
PAUL ELLIMAN

PROJECT DESCRIPTION
'READING TYPOGRAPHY WRITING LANGUAGE. AN INVITATION TO READ BUT NOT TO WRITE: ANALPHABET, A COLLECTION OF THINGS THAT UNINTENTIONALLY REVEAL ASPECTS OF THE FORM OF LANGUAGE BUT CONCEAL THE ACT OF LANGUAGE, EMPHASISED BY THEIR APPARENT NAMELESSNESS. IN FACT, NAMING THEM RECALLS THE CLASSICAL DIGNITY OF ORAL LANGUAGE; ESCUTCHEONS, GROMMETS, CORE-WINDING, CURTAIN WEIGHTS, COINS, STONES, BUTTONS, RUBBER WASHERS, A POZI-DRIVE, A U-BOLT, AN O-RING, LINKS, BOTTLE-TOPS, CUP-HOOKS, CLAMPS, TRIMS, SEALERS, CLIPS, BRACKETS, SWEETS, KEYS, STRINGS, SPRINGS, NUTS, METAL, STONE, ETC.'

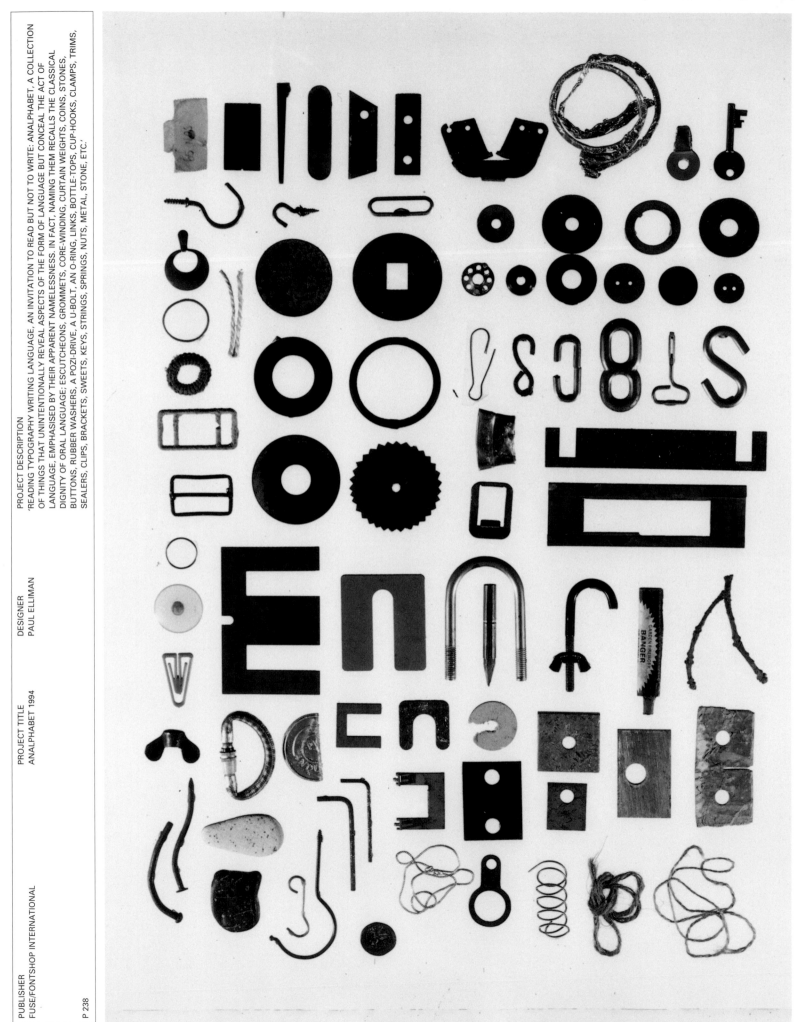

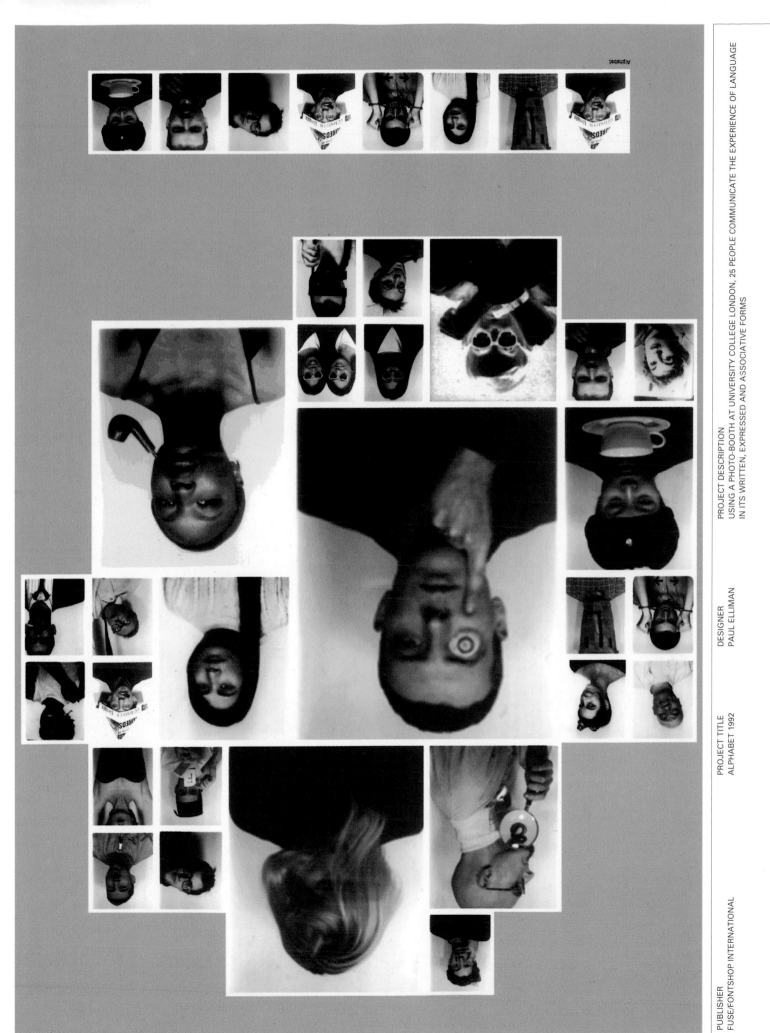

Alphabet

PUBLISHER
FUSE/FONTSHOP INTERNATIONAL

PROJECT TITLE
ALPHABET 1992

DESIGNER
PAUL ELLIMAN

PROJECT DESCRIPTION
USING A PHOTO-BOOTH AT UNIVERSITY COLLEGE LONDON, 25 PEOPLE COMMUNICATE THE EXPERIENCE OF LANGUAGE
IN ITS WRITTEN, EXPRESSED AND ASSOCIATIVE FORMS

P.239

ARTIST
JEAN-MICHEL JARRE

CAPTIONS
1   2

P 240 AND 241 (PREVIOUS)

CLIENT
FRENCH GOVERNMENT

ARTIST
JEAN-MICHEL JARRE

CAPTIONS
1, 2   3   4

5

6

7

CLIENT
CITY OF HOUSTON

P 242 AND 243

PROJECT DESCRIPTION
FIFTEEN TOWNS AWASH WITH LIGHT AND SOUND AS
PART OF A STUNNING AND UNFORGETTABLE EUROPEAN
TOUR

PROJECT DESCRIPTION
CLOSING OF BICENTENNIAL OF THE FRENCH REVOLUTION
CELEBRATIONS

PHOTOGRAPHY
SERGE DELCROIX

PHOTOGRAPHY
A FEVRIER
ALAIN BOU
E BONNIER-BEREWISE

PHOTOGRAPHY
A DE WILDENBERG

PROJECT TITLE
MONT SAINT-MICHEL
EUROPE IN CONCERT
THE 1993 TOUR

1, 2

PROJECT TITLE
PARIS - LA DEFENSE
A CITY IN CONCERT

1, 2, 3   4

PROJECT TITLE
RENDEZ-VOUS HOUSTON

5, 6, 7

'IMAGINATION AND FICTION MAKE UP MORE THAN THREE-QUARTERS OF OUR REAL LIVES.'

SIMONE WEIL

P 246 AND 247 (244 AND 245 PREVIOUS)

CLIENT
FORD MOTOR COMPANY

PROJECT TITLE
FORD MOTOR SHOW EXHIBITIONS

DESIGN COMPANY
IMAGINATION

PROJECT DESCRIPTION
A 'SPHERE OF INNOVATION' ENVELOPS VISITORS IN THE WORLD OF THE BRAND AND PROVIDES THE FOCUS FOR FORD'S 1992 PAN-EUROPEAN MOTOR SHOW EXHIBITION PROGRAMME

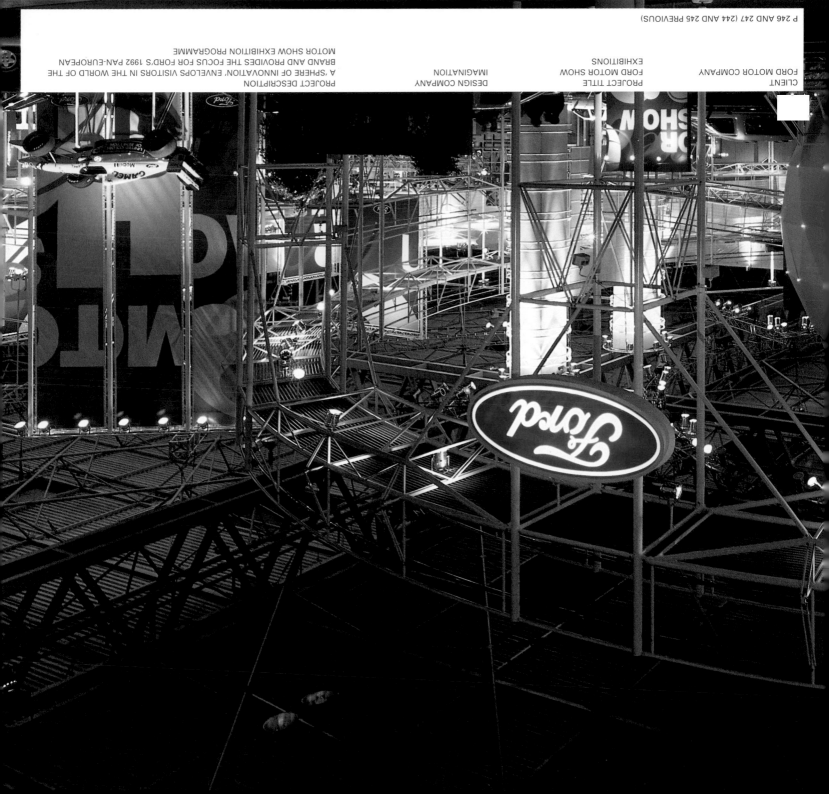

CLIENT
FORD MOTOR COMPANY

PROJECT TITLE
FORD AT THE LONDON
MOTOR SHOW 1993

DESIGN COMPANY
IMAGINATION

PROJECT DESCRIPTION
ACROSS EUROPE, FORD HAS LED THE WAY IN TRANSFORMING MOTOR SHOWS INTO EXCITING, IMAGINATIVE AND INTER-
ACTIVE LEISURE EVENTS FOR THE CONSUMER. THIS INNOVATIVE WALK-THROUGH EXPERIENCE, THEMED AROUND 'SAFETY
AND TECHNOLOGY', WAS DEVISED FOR THE 1993 LONDON MOTOR SHOW. HOUSED IN A COMPLETELY ENCLOSED 1,457 SQ
METRE SPACE, THE FORD EXPERIENCE COMBINED THEATRICAL TECHNIQUES WITH AUDIO-VISUAL TECHNOLOGY, GRAPHICS
AND VIDEO

P 248 AND 249

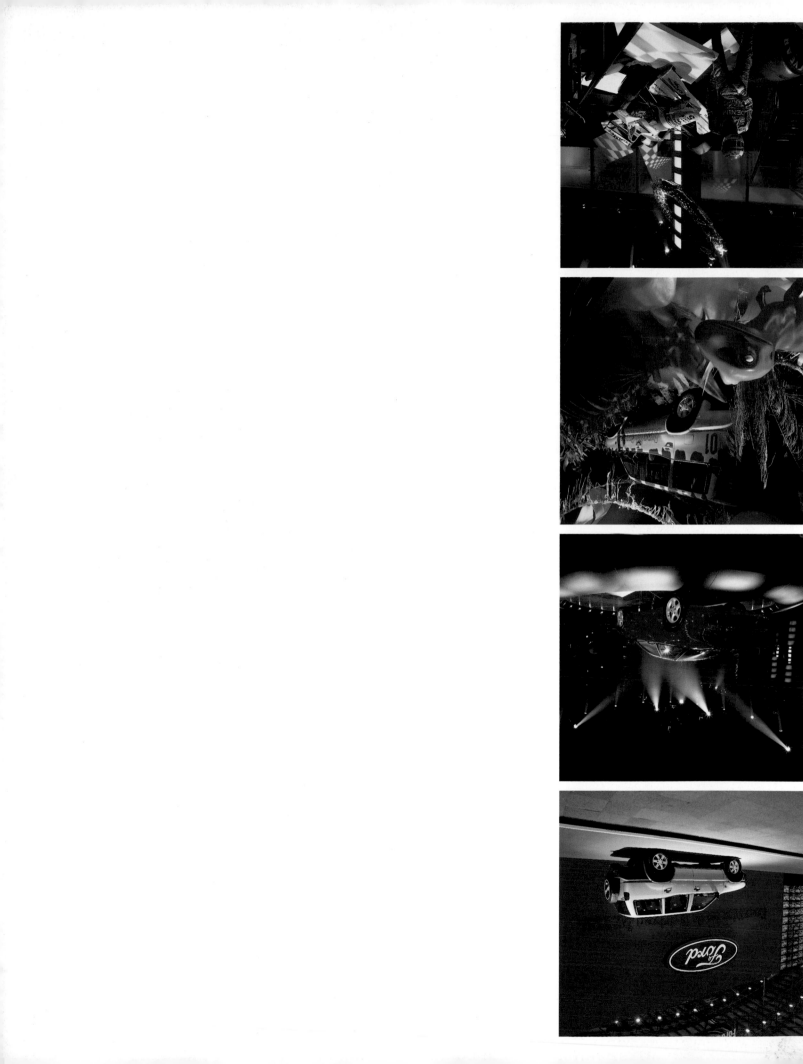

P 250 AND 251

FILM ARCHITECT
ROLF ZEHETBAUER

CLIENT
BMW AG

PROJECT
BMW MUSEUM

ARCHITECT
PROFESSOR KARL SCHWANZER

PROJECT DESCRIPTION
BMW'S HEADQUARTERS AND THE BMW MUSEUM, MUNICH 1973

AMLUX CENTRE PROVIDES A PHYSICAL
EXPRESSION OF THE TOYOTA BRAND.

ITS SIX FLOORS INVITE THE VISITOR TO
EXPLORE THE WORLD OF TOYOTA
THROUGH A BEWILDERING ARRAY OF
INTERACTIVE, INFORMATIVE AND ENTER-
TAINING ENVIRONMENTS AND PRESEN-
TATIONS. THESE INCLUDE A HOLOGRAPHIC
FACTORY, FUTURE CAR DESIGN STUDIO,
TECHNOLOGY GALLERY, SURROUND
SOUND THEATRE, BODY SONIC AND
AROMA SYSTEMS, MEDIA STATIONS AND
A LIVE EVENTS FLOOR FOR CONFERENCES,
PARTIES, DINING AND CONCERTS.

TOYOTA'S AMLUX CENTRE IS A TESTIMONY
TO THE POWER OF DESIGN TO CREATE
DIALOGUE AND BUILD RELATIONSHIPS
THROUGH INDUCED EXPERIENCES.

CLIENT
TOYOTA MOTOR
CORPORATION

DESIGN COMPANY
DENTSU INC

ARCHITECTS
NIKKEN SEKKEI LTD
TAKENAKA CORPORATION

PROJECT DESCRIPTION
TOYOTA AUTO SALON AMLUX, TOKYO

P 252 AND 253

ARTIST
RICHARD WILSON

TITLE
20:50

COURTESY
SAATCHI COLLECTION, LONDON

PROJECT DESCRIPTION
20:50 COMPRISES OF A SHALLOW STEEL CONTAINER WITH AN INSERTED WALKWAY THAT ENABLES THE VIEWER TO ENTER THE INSTALLATION. THE CONTAINER IS FILLED WITH SUMP OIL WHICH ACTS LIKE A REFLECTING POOL. THE DENSITY OF THE OIL MAKES IT IMPOSSIBLE TO ESTIMATE ITS DEPTH

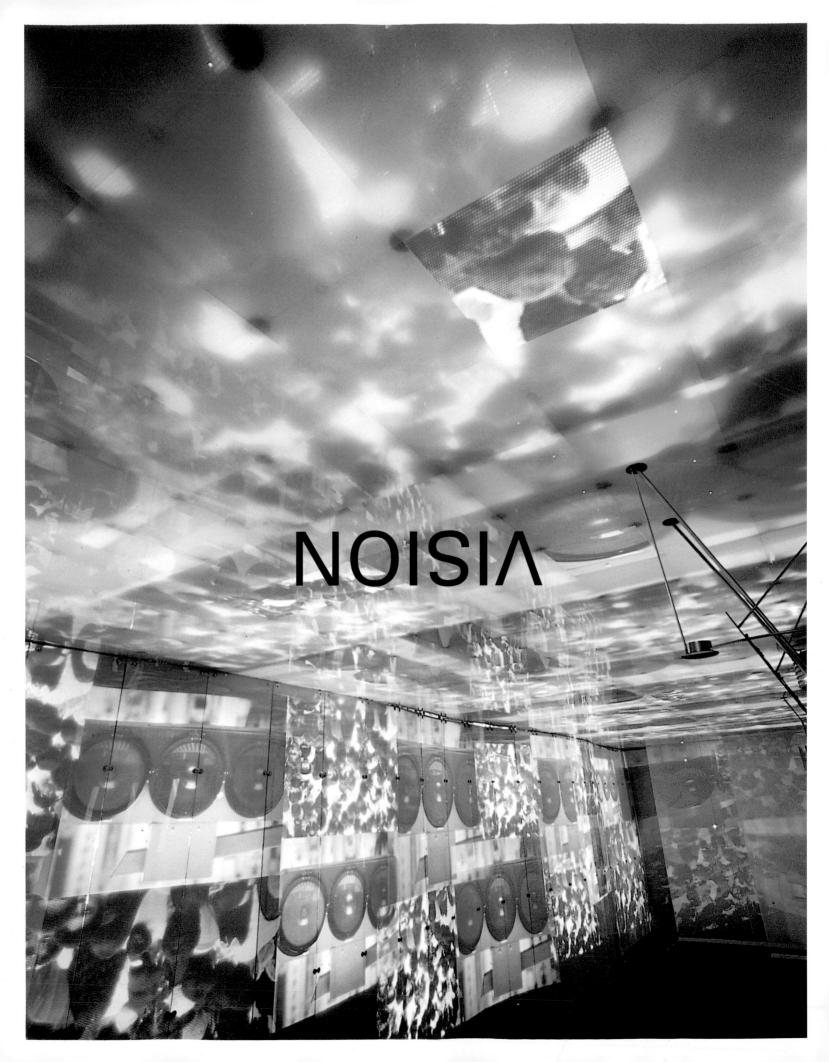

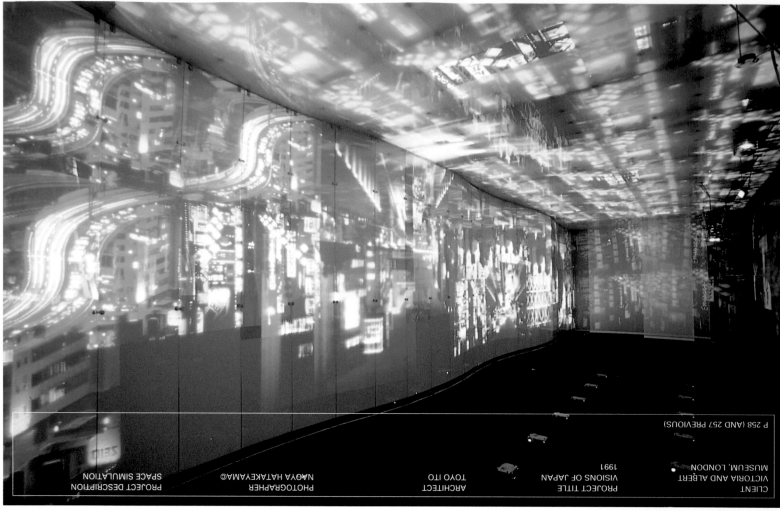

CLIENT	PROJECT TITLE	ARCHITECT	PHOTOGRAPHER	PROJECT DESCRIPTION
VICTORIA AND ALBERT MUSEUM, LONDON	VISIONS OF JAPAN 1991	TOYO ITO	NAOYA HATAKEYAMA©	SPACE SIMULATION

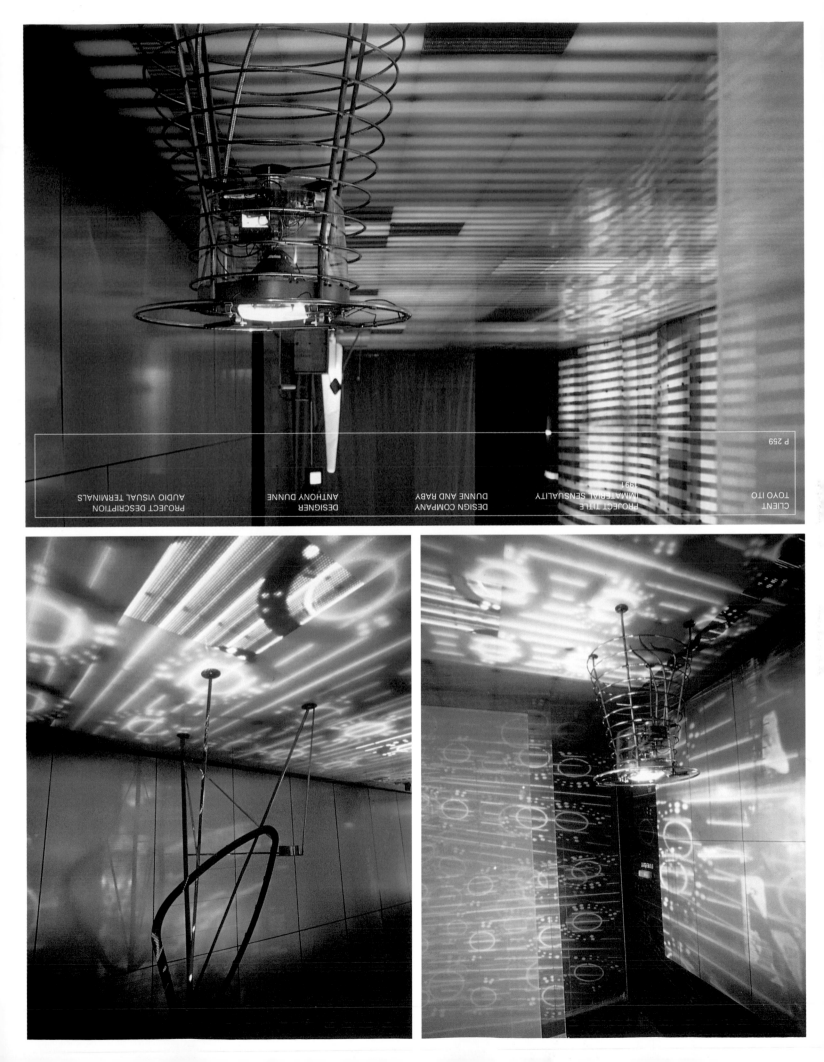

CLIENT
TOYO ITO

PROJECT TITLE
IMMATERIAL SENSUALITY
1991

DESIGN COMPANY
DUNNE AND RABY

DESIGNER
ANTHONY DUNNE

PROJECT DESCRIPTION
AUDIO VISUAL TERMINALS

p 259

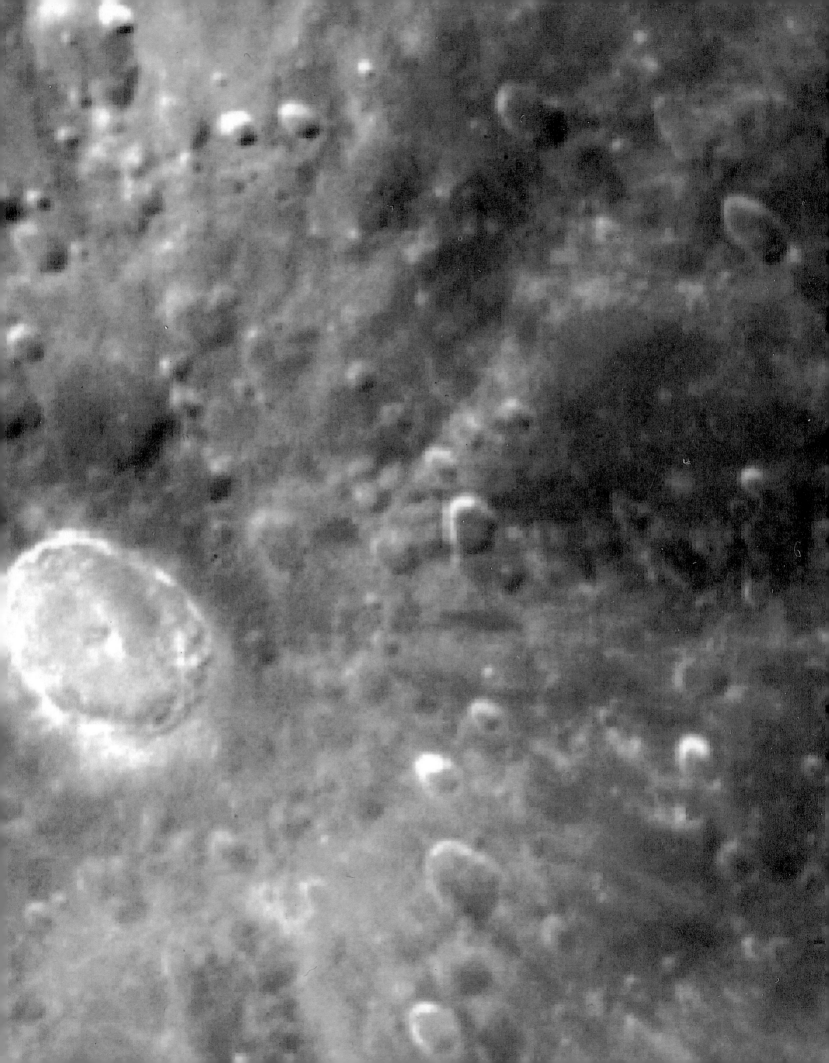

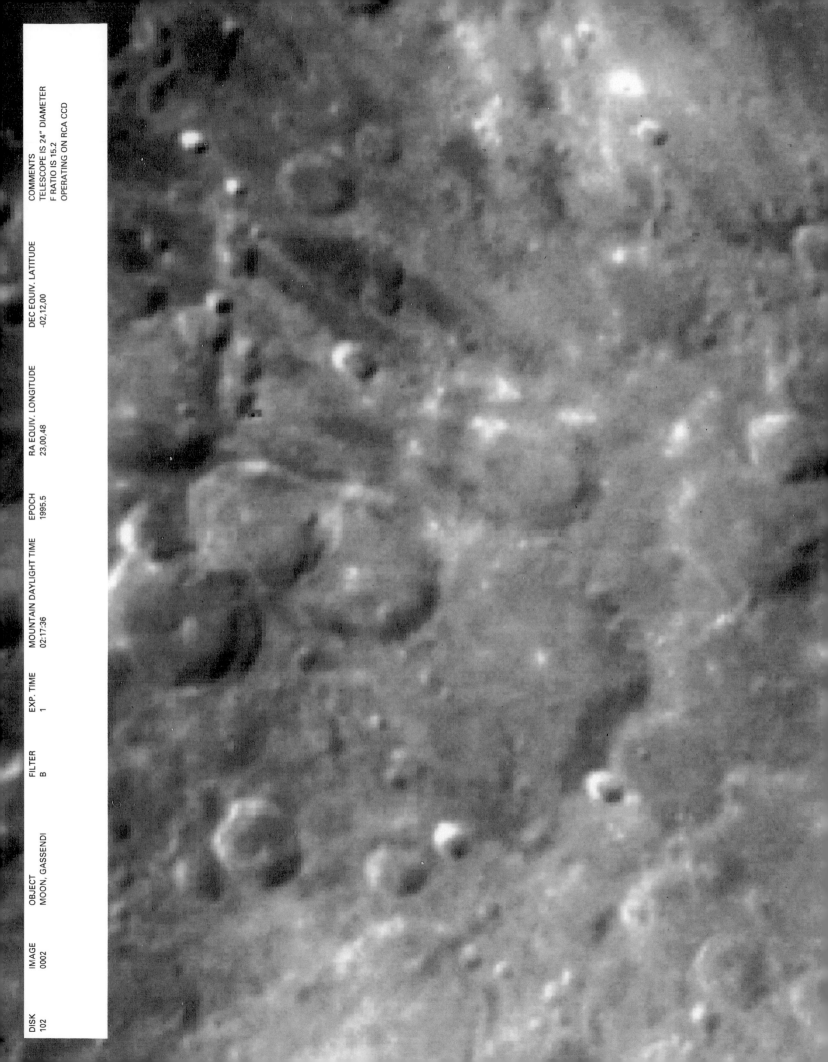

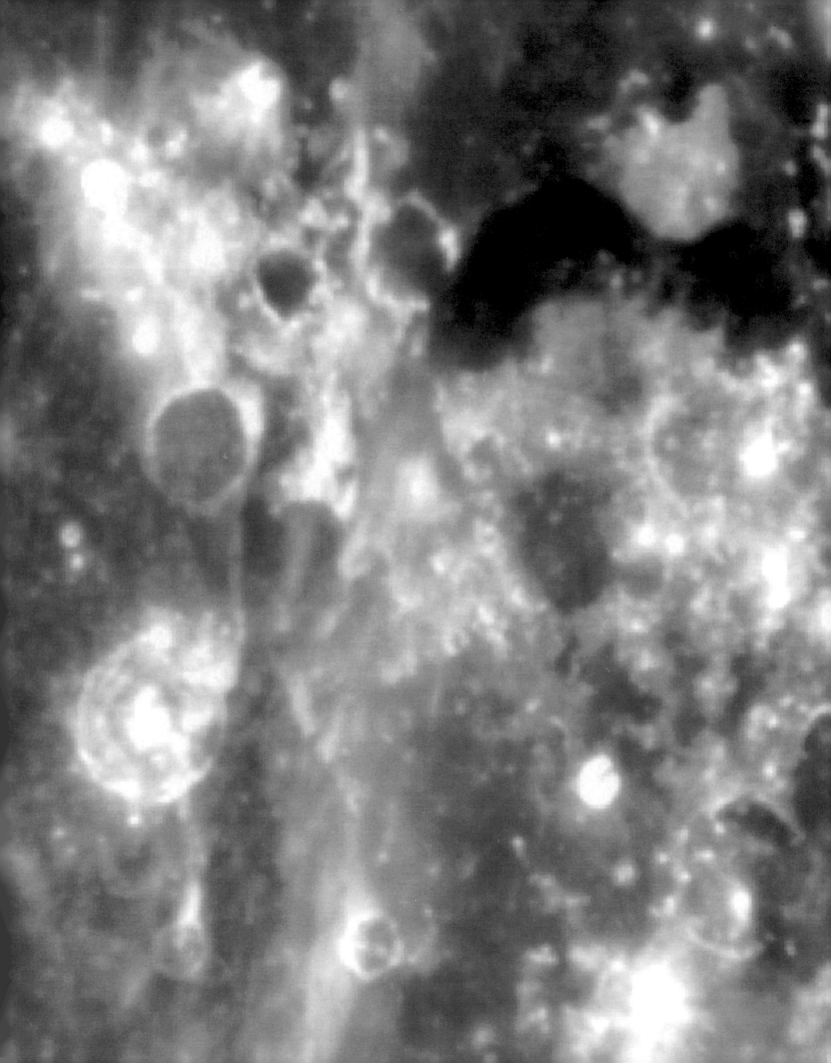

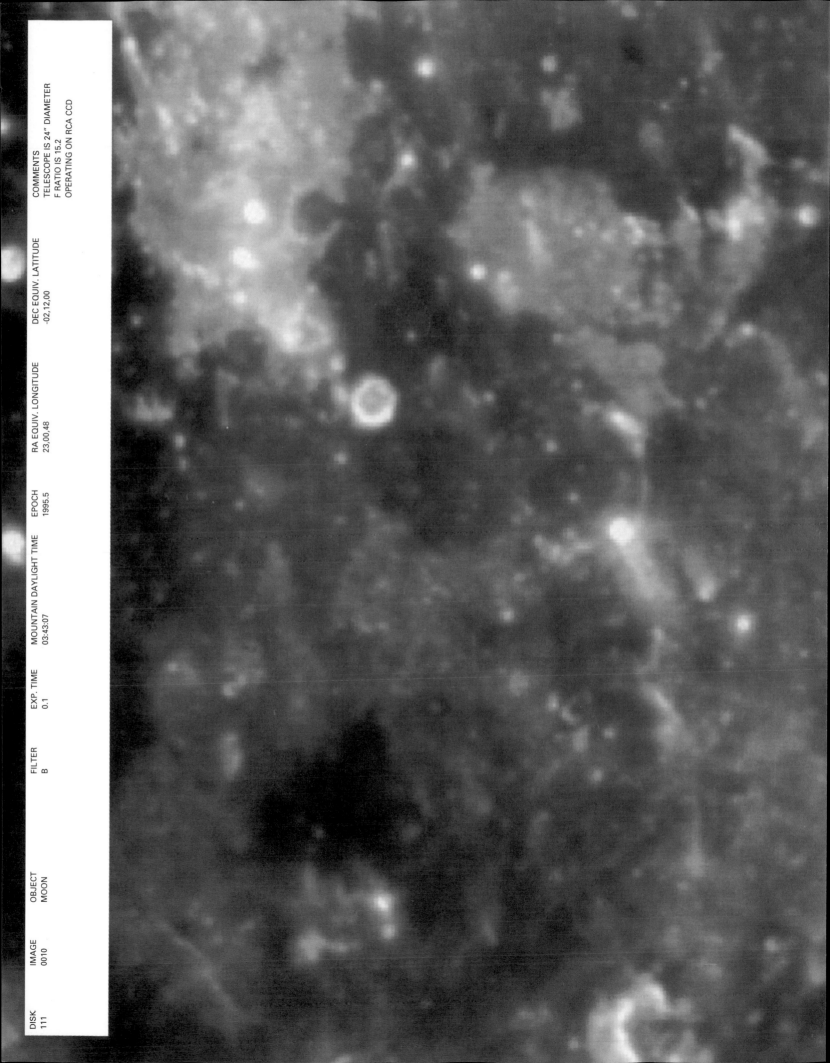

DISK
111

IMAGE
0010

OBJECT
MOON

FILTER
B

EXP. TIME
0.1

MOUNTAIN DAYLIGHT TIME
03:43:07

EPOCH
1995.5

RA EQUIV. LONGITUDE
23,00,48

DEC EQUIV. LATITUDE
-02,12,00

COMMENTS
TELESCOPE IS 24" DIAMETER
F RATIO IS 15.2
OPERATING ON RCA CCD

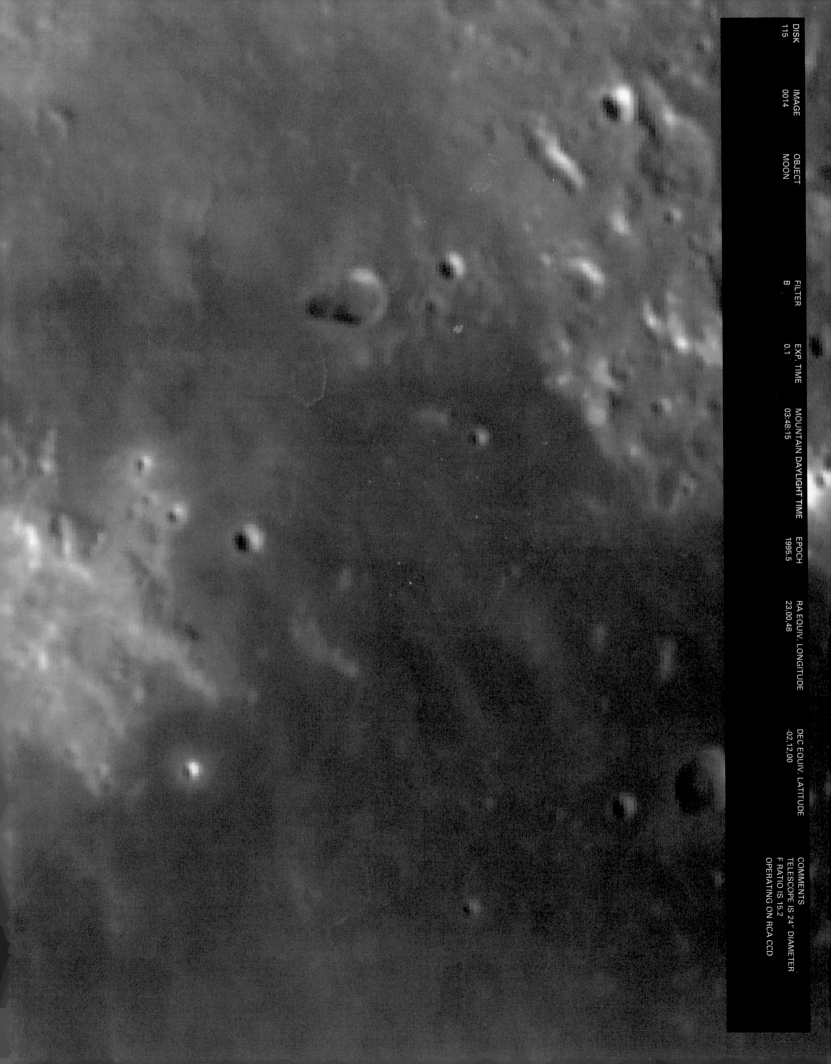

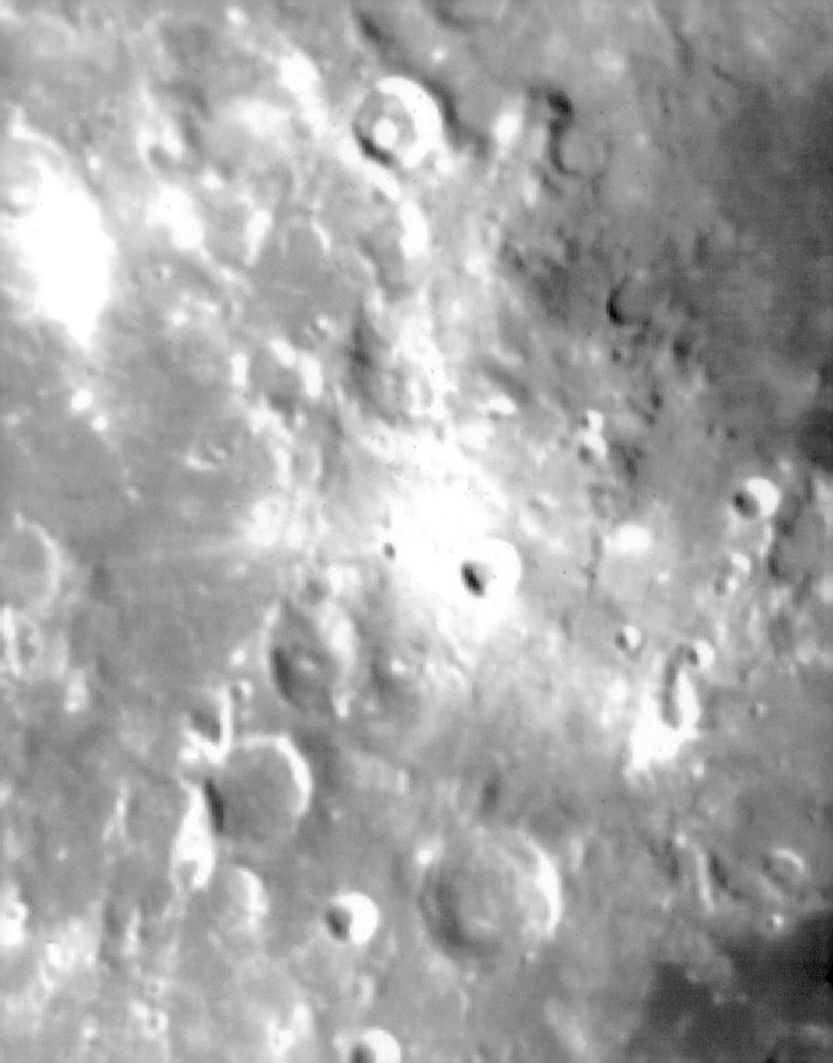